HURON COUNTY PUBLIC LIBRARY

SO-BJF-301

HURON COUNTY LIBRARY

2 008 082597 7

DISCARD

60004

j971.06   Harris, Jeanette.
Har   Canada; the land and its people. London,
        Macdonald Educational, 1976.
            61 p. ill., maps. (Macdonald countries)
        (A Silver Burdett International Library
        selection)

            1. Canada - Social life and customs.
        I. Title.
        0382061101 1b   1188038 LC

Canada

Editor Susan Ward
Design Patrick Frean
Picture Research Maggie Colbeck
Production Rosemary Bishop
Consultant J. L. Ortman
Illustrations Ron Hayward Associates
John Shackell
Tony Payne
Maps Matthews and Taylor Associates

First published 1976
Macdonald Educational Ltd.
Holywell House, Worship Street
London EC2A 2EN

© Macdonald Educational
Limited 1976
ISBN 0-382-06110-1

Photographic Sources Key to positions
of illustrations: *(T)*top, *(C)*centre,
*(B)*bottom, *(L)*left, *(R)*right.
Alpha *49(TR)*, Camera Press
13(TR), *29(T)*, (Karsh of Ottawa)
36(BC), Canadian Broadcasting
Corporation *26(T)*, *36-37(B)*, *37(BL)*.
J. Alan Cash *14(B)*, *15(TL) (CR)*, *24(B)*,
25(TR), *28(BL)*, *28-29(T)*, *43(TR)*,
44(TL), *45(C)*, *46-47(B)*, *50(BL)*. Daily
Telegraph Colour Library *15(BL)*,
16(BL), *35(BL)*, *45(BL)*. Glyn Davis
15(BL), *18-19(BC)*, *20(T)*, *23(BR)*,
25(BL). Eatons, Toronto *31(BL)*, Robert
Estall *8-9(C)*, *9(BR)*, *12(BL)*, *13(BC)*,
18(TC), *22(BL)(BR)*, *26(B)*, *31(R)*,
33(C), *34(B)*, *35(BL)*, *43(BL)*, *46(TL)*,
52-53(B), *53(BR)*. Tom Hanley *33(R)*,
38-39(B), *39(TL)*, *42(BR)*, *51(BL)*.
Robert Harding *9(TL)*, *13(TL)*, *16(BR)*,
16-17(T), *35(TC)*, *40-41(C)*. Information
Canada *34-35(T)*, *37(TR)*, *39(TR)*,
41(TR), *51(BR)*. Joyce Jason *9(TR)*,
20(BC), *21(TL)(TR)*, *31(BR)*, *45(TR)*,
47(TL), *52(TC)*, *53(TL)*. Keystone
29(BR). Kobal Collection *13(BL)*.
Macdonald Educational *49(BR)*. Rob
MacIntyre *30(BL)*, *40(B)*, *53(TR)*.
McMichael Canadian Collection,
Kleinburg Ontario *37(TL)*. Manitoba
Government Information *19(TR)*. Mary
Evans Picture Library *49(TL)*. Ontario
Ministry of Information *45(BR)*. Popper
47(TR). Public Archives of Canada
8(BL), *27(TL)(R)*, *48(BL)*. Radio
Times Hulton Picture Library *27(BR)*,
49(BC). G. R. Roberts *17(BL)(TR)*,
18(BL), *23(BL)*, *30(BR)*, *33(TL)*,
39(BR), *42(BC)*, *43(C)*, *44(BL)*. Royal
Ontario Museum *36(L)*, SEF *14(TC)*,
16(TL), *31(TL)*, *43(BR)*, *44(BR)*.
Spectrum *19(TL)*, *21(BR)*, *36(L)*,
38(BL), *41(TC)*, *46(BL)*. Toronto Star
(Macpherson) *28(TL)*, (Bickerstaff)
52(BL), ZEFA *14(C)*, *17(BR)*, *28-29(B)*.

Cover: The Mounties—or Royal
Canadian Mounted Police—present one
of Canada's most stalwart images.
Established in 1873, they supervised the
settlement of the western provinces and
the territories. Today they enforce federal
laws throughout Canada. *Pictor*

Endpaper: "Breadbasket of the World"
—the rich farmlands of Saskatchewan
seem endless. These wooden grain depots
at Grand Coulee line the railway
which stretches across the fertile plains to
the Great Lakes. *G. R. Roberts*

Page 6: Medicine Lake in Jasper
National Park, Alberta. The province's
national parks—including Banff, Jasper,
Elk Island, Waterton Lakes and Wood
Buffalo—are among the wonders of the
Northern Hemisphere. Breath-taking
scenery and abundant wildlife make them
favourites of naturalists, photographers
and holiday-makers. *Textes et images*

Published in the United
States by Silver Burdett
Company, Morristown, N. J.
1977 Printing

Library of Congress
Catalog Card No. 77-70185

Canada

the land and its people

Jeanette Harris

60004

NOV 18 '80

GODERICH BRANCH LIBRARY

Macdonald Educational

Contents

The first Canadians

East comes west

In 1967 Canada celebrated her first hundred years as a nation. In the same year, archaeological investigations indicated that the country was inhabited at least 30,000 years earlier. These first Canadians followed big game to North America from Siberia, over what was once a land bridge across today's Bering Sea. Some remained nomadic hunters, while others led a more settled life farming and fishing.

Who knows the real "discoverer" of America? Over 1500 years ago Chinese writers told stories about the northern lands of Tahan and Fusang, across the great ocean. The first Europeans to reach North America were Vikings from Iceland and Greenland. In 1000 Leif the Lucky was blown off course to the Labrador coast and possibly Nova Scotia. He and his men enjoyed themselves in "Vinland" and Thorfinn Karlsefni followed in their wake, establishing a brief settlement.

The Kingdom of the Saguenay

A few centuries later other explorers followed, prompted by curiosity, dreams of empire, missionary zeal and visions of a North-West Passage to the riches of the Orient. But less grandiose demands for cod and for beaver pelts kept them coming. In 1497 John Cabot discovered Canada's east coast and the great fishing banks. In 1504 St. John's, Newfoundland, was established as an English fishing base.

Jacques Cartier pushed farther in 1534. At first unimpressed with this "land God gave to Cain", he changed his mind after visiting the Indian towns of Stadacona (Quebec city) and Hochelaga (near Montreal). Rapids barred his path onward and he turned back reluctantly, dreaming of India and the mythical Kingdom of the Saguenay.

Later in 1608 Samuel de Champlain, the first Governor of New France, founded its capital, Quebec, after a less successful attempt at Port Royal. With settlement came the Indians' downfall. European diseases, guns, liquor and indeed Indian dependence on European ways, as well as their own feuds, all contributed to it. Ironically the Indians had taught the Europeans how to survive in Canada.

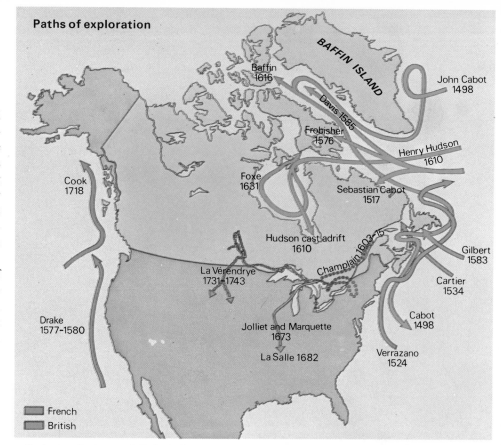

Paths of exploration

French
British

▲ Curiosity, Cathay and Christianity, trade and empire all attracted explorers. In 1942, the RCMP schooner *St. Roch* under Henry Larsen finally traversed the Northwest Passage.

▼ Samuel de Champlain, the Father of New France, explored as far as Lake Nipissing, seeking a new route to the wealth of the Orient.

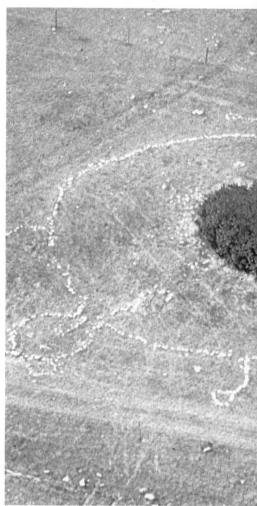

▲ A reconstructed fur press at Fort Edmonton. Hudson's Bay Company posts spread law, order and British title as far as the Pacific.

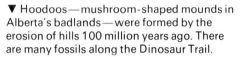

▶ Jacques Cartier discovered the mainland. During a hard winter in Quebec, his ill-fed crew were saved from scurvy by the Indian remedy of medicinal tea made from bark.

▼ This giant 135-foot turtle effigy was built of stones near Minton on the prairies. Turtles were sacred as symbols of bravery to tribes like the Saulteaux.

▼ Hoodoos—mushroom-shaped mounds in Alberta's badlands—were formed by the erosion of hills 100 million years ago. There are many fossils along the Dinosaur Trail.

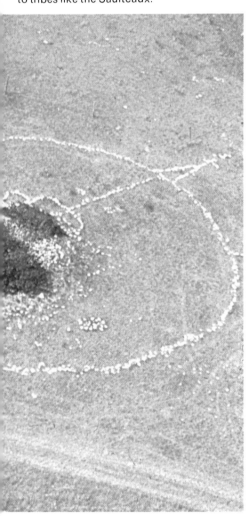

From sea to sea

Manitoba

Newfoundland

▶ The DEW or Distant Early Warning line in the north went into operation in 1957. It is controlled by both Canadian and U.S. air defense.

YUKON

NORTHWEST TERRITORIES

Yellowknife

BRITISH

COLUMBIA

ALBERTA

SASKATCHEWAN

Victoria

Regina

▲ Ogopogo (a distant relation of the Loch Ness monster) reputedly lurks in Okanagan Lake, in the heart of British Columbia's fruitful valley.

Saskatchewan

Alberta

British Columbia

Wide open spaces

There is room to breathe in Canada. With 9.8 million square kilometres (3.8 million square miles), it is the second largest country in the world, larger than the U.S. or Europe. Seven of the world's 24 time zones cross six dramatically different regions. Even since World War II, aerial survey has found unknown land at the top of Hudson's Bay. Only one-third of the country has been developed, however, and most of the relatively small population of 22 million live within 100 miles of the U.S. border. Yet the land's vastness is always at the back of a Canadian's mind and remains oddly reassuring.

Ten provinces, two territories

From the Atlantic to the Pacific stretches a land of extremes in temperature and terrain. In the East lie the Maritime or Atlantic provinces, whose newest member, Newfoundland, only decided to join Canada in 1948 after two votes.

Crags and inlets soon give way to the more fertile land of the St. Lawrence area, the most densely populated and industrialized part of Canada. Here—between Canada's oldest city, Quebec, and Lake Huron—Montreal and Toronto, the two largest cities, preside over their rich hinterlands. Past the rock barrier of the Canadian Shield lie the endless grain lands of the prairies, and farther west still are the splendid Rockies. The mild climate of British Columbia's matchless coast is a striking contrast to that of the Yukon and the Northwest Territories, Canada's last frontier in the north.

This landscape has posed immense natural barriers to development, as well as offering many inducements. Its features run north and south rather than east and west; a continental pull often facilitating contact with the United States instead of the rest of Canada. British ties, the French presence and the St. Lawrence River system have all counteracted this pull. Perhaps the very obstacles faced by Canadians have ensured their cooperation.

Ontario

Nova Scotia

Prince Edward Island

New Brunswick

Quebec

BAFFIN ISLAND

Ungava Peninsula

Hudson

Bay

Churchill

MANITOBA

▼ St. Pierre and Miquelon, small fishing islands off Newfoundland, are the only colonies left in North America.

NEWFOUNDLAND

St. Johns

QUEBEC

ONTARIO

Kapuskasing

Prince Edward Is.

NEW BRUNSWICK

NOVA SCOTIA

Montreal

◄ The Bay of Fundy has the highest tides in the world. Rushing through St. John harbour, they create the amazing Reversing Falls.

Toronto

The Yukon

Northwest Territories

► The 100-mile long Manitoulin Island in Lake Huron is the world's largest freshwater island, with over 100 lakes of its own.

The Canadian influence

"He's a lumberjack and he's okay—!"

Mention Canada to a foreigner and he automatically thinks of robust lumberjacks, romantic Mounties, vast natural resources, the Niagara Falls, French separatists, hockey hijinks, and the U.S. Some may remark that several relatives emigrated there and were too snowbound to return. But Expo '67 and the 1976 Olympics are publicizing the country more, and Canadians themselves are spreading: the red maple leaf on so many tourists isn't the international hitch-hiking sign, but the Canadian flag!

A peaceable kingdom

Canadians have achieved a great deal quietly. In medicine they have done their share of heart transplants and both Toronto and McGill universities have international reputations in biochemistry and neuro-chemistry. The discovery of insulin was one of medicine's greatest achievements.

Although some would wish Canada's defences improved, in World War II she ranked third in naval strength and fourth in air power among the Allies. She was also a founding member of NATO and a joint member of NORAD in air defense with the U.S. But her real interest lies in the U.N., and the Canadian temperament is suited to mediation. Her own cultural diversity may yet be an example to countries increasingly fragmented by internal divisions.

▲ Canadian lumberjacks are famous for their plaid jackets and log-cutting contests, particularly in B.C. where the thousand year-old Douglas Fir has grown as high as 300 feet.

Leaders in science and industry

Marshall McLuhan, a Toronto professor, brought media into the arts with *The Medium is the Message*.

Sir Frederick Banting discovered insulin against diabetes with Dr. Charles Best in 1921—a major breakthrough in modern medicine.

The Rt. Hon. Lord Thomson of Fleet heads a transatlantic newspaper empire and the Thomson organization.

◄ Canada Geese are a well-known species and their migratory flight patterns in V formation are familiar sights. Jack Miner, a Canadian naturalist, began banding ducks in 1904 and led studies in migratory habits.

▼ Pierre Trudeau's charismatic charm is equally at ease in French- and English-speaking Canada. A dapper PM, he cuts quite a dash abroad. At home his hopes for a new society have met with mixed response.

▲ Habitat is a permanent housing complex shown at the world's fair in Montreal. Expo '67 was a coup for Montreal and a centennial morale boost for Canada.

► Canadian Air Force exercises for men and women help to keep the world fit—and occasionally even Canadians!

▼ Wild rice or manomin is a delicacy which costs more, but yields 4 times its volume after cooking. Harvested by teams of Indians in canoes, it grows up to 8' high.

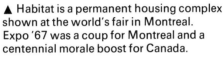

▲ The Royal Canadian Mounted Police rival lumberjacks as the Canadian image abroad. Mounties always get their man—or woman! —especially in movies like *Rosemarie*. Its 9,000 members are highly respected.

Land of the living

▶ Whitehorse, headquarters for the Royal Canadian Mounted Police, is a thriving young city of goldrush fame. Here summer sunlight lasts more than 20 hours a day, while autumn evenings are brilliantly lit by the *aurora borealis*.

▲ Vancouver is Canada's third largest city. It is blessed with a great harbour, an incomparable setting and a mild, wet climate which keeps it green all year. Canada's largest aquarium is in Stanley Park and Vancouverites are great outdoorsmen. Skiing in nearby mountains or sailing on English Bay are favourite pastimes. Though her inhabitants may feel somewhat cut off from the east, the rest of snowbound Canada has always had a soft spot for this city.

▶ Chateau Frontenac can be seen from every point in Quebec City, and even twenty miles away. This is one of Canada's oldest and most picturesque cities. More French than Montreal, it is the only walled city on the continent. Here in the Upper Town, the old Citadel guards the headwaters of the St. Lawrence, while in the Lower Town by the riverbank, are the winding streets of the *vieux quartier*, or old neighbourhood.

Capitals and cottages

It is predicted that by the year 2000, 90% of all Canadians will live in cities. Already more than half live in twenty-one cities of more than 100,000. Yet many smaller centres remain distinctively Canadian: wooden Maritime fishing ports, Quebec villages dominated by a spire, sleepy small towns in southern Ontario, clusters of country cottages brought to life every summer, isolated communities with their busy social calendars.

The commercial hub

Canadian cities may seem typically North American. Yet each has its own character, and all are lively by day and safe by night. Montreal, Canada's largest city, is the second largest French-speaking city in the world and famous for its nightlife, modern centre and decorative metro. An exciting mixture of English and French, it has hosted the World's Fair, "Expo '67", and the 1976 Olympics.

Toronto, its more sedate rival, boasts an antiseptic subway, a space age city hall, the highest unsupported structure in the world, and the Canadian National Exhibition, a giant country fair remembered nostalgically by generations of children as the "Ex".

Stephen Leacock, Canada's great humorist, once remarked that to a Canadian, going West is like the quest for the Holy Grail. Every winter, Torontonians dream of retiring to mild Vancouver with its Mediterranean attractions. Their children usually get there first.

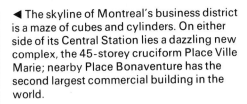

◄ The skyline of Montreal's business district is a maze of cubes and cylinders. On either side of its Central Station lies a dazzling new complex, the 45-storey cruciform Place Ville Marie; nearby Place Bonaventure has the second largest commercial building in the world.

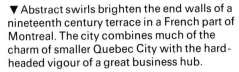

▼ Abstract swirls brighten the end walls of a nineteenth century terrace in a French part of Montreal. The city combines much of the charm of smaller Quebec City with the hard-headed vigour of a great business hub.

◄ The Canadian National Tower is an unmistakable Toronto landmark. Built to provide improved radio and television signals for the Toronto area, it is the world's tallest free-standing structure.

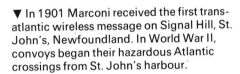

▼ In 1901 Marconi received the first trans-atlantic wireless message on Signal Hill, St. John's, Newfoundland. In World War II, convoys began their hazardous Atlantic crossings from St. John's harbour.

Peaks, plains and ice

East is east

Although Canadian society today is largely urbanized, the land is still an inescapable influence. The changing face of its seasons moves people in an uniquely Canadian rhythm, especially in those areas where man is still very much the interloper.

In the East, confronting the Atlantic, is the Appalachian or Acadian region, with its picturesque, craggy shoreline and mountain ranges created 350 million years ago, the home of fishermen and trappers. Farther inland, in the heart of Canada one of the largest group of lakes in the world provides Canada's major fresh water and hydroelectric resource. Dominating the Hudson Bay and half of Canada is the Precambrian or Canadian Shield, the rugged plateau once called "Laurentian monster".

And West is west

Rolling hypnotically to the West, the Interior Plains rise 3,000 feet in three stages to Alberta. Beneath hide many minerals, and oil exploration is in full swing. Great flocks of migratory birds rest here on their way south, while deer, moose, caribou and black bears thrive. The powerful grizzly bear roams the rough terrain of Alberta and B.C. whose big horn sheep attract hunters. Hunting and conservation are equally successful ventures. On the west coast, the plentiful salmon always return to spawn and die in the same creek in which they were born. Finally, Canadian Rangers keep an eye on the far north with its great oil and mineral potential, the land of the midnight sun.

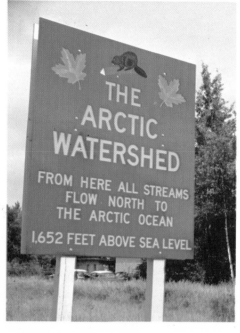

▲ This sign near Fort William marks the Arctic Watershed; all water flows north from this latitude. The Mackenzie River, Canada's main wilderness artery, empties into the Arctic Ocean after 1,120 miles.

▼ Eskimo igloos probably developed from snow blocks piled around skin tents. Warm inside, they are often smokey from burning blubber.

▲ Most of the eastern Northwest Territories is north of the tree line. Above this is a windswept tundra studded with lakes—the home of seals, polar bear and Arctic char.

◄ With their spikey peaks and blue-green lakes, the Rockies are the best-known of the three high ranges in the Western Cordilleras. Cataracts, glaciers and orchards are superb.

▼ Life on the smaller subsistence farms in the Canadian Shield can be difficult. The owner of these stony acres must work part-time in the local saw mill to survive.

◄ The population density in the prairie provinces is 5 per square mile. Not for nothing is Canada called "Breadbasket of the World".

▼ Fleet's in, in this small Newfoundland bay. The sea is a hard mistress, but about 80,000 work in Canada's fishing industry, which ranks first in the world.

Family life

▶ St. Anne de Beaupré is a famous shrine 21 miles east of Quebec City. It was founded in 1650 by grateful French fishermen after a stormy Atlantic crossing. Today there are about 10 million Roman Catholics in Canada. Urbanization and the elimination of the church's dominance of state education in Quebec has weakened Catholicism's secular influence in that province. But it is still a strong force in French-Canadian family life.

▼ Canadians are a family-orientated people. Parents and children usually start the day together with breakfast, and the evening meal is spent discussing everyone's adventures. Weekends see packed cars heading for the wilds.

All in the family

Suburban life does not differ much from other Western countries. Canadians work hard and play hard. Standards of living are high, and detached homes and at least one car are normal expectations. More wives are returning to work and Canadian husbands are usually helpful and generous partners. The law encourages equal opportunities. Children help with chores and may have part-time jobs to increase their weekly allowance. After school, parents drive them to hockey practice or other activities like piano lessons. Grandparents often visit at weekends, which are dominated by shopping, gardening, the Saturday night date for teenagers and "Hockey Night in Canada" on T.V. Canadian families are generally conservative in their entertainment tastes. Yet they enjoy holidays in cottages, camps or the Caribbean.

Although some city congregations are declining, Canadians have traditionally been churchgoing people—except perhaps in summer! The local church is usually a social centre. Young people everywhere are less reverent about any establishment. In Quebec the "Quiet Revolution" has changed many of the old values. Even Toronto's Protestant Orange Parade mostly attracts local Italians. If Canada often seems like a secular society with few otherworldly con-considerations, it is because Canadians today are tolerant and easy-going about their neighbour's beliefs.

Day in the life of a suburban family

◄ Eskimos adjusted remarkably well to a severe environment. Today, many work in successful co-operatives, and most live in modern government housing.

▼ Prize bull and proud owner at a beef show. The limited free time enjoyed by farm children is often devoted to raising such "pets".

► A typical Fort William suburb. Nearly two-thirds of the population live in single detached houses. The average has five rooms. With rising real estate costs, jointly-owned apartments, or condominiums, are becoming popular.

▼ Snowed in ! Shovelling the driveway is a familiar Canadian exercise in winter. The entire family takes turns in building muscle.

Education for all

One quarter of public spending

Canadians place great value on education and the cost is high. Each province manages its own, and the quality is generally excellent. Children must go to school from the age of 6 to 14, depending on the province. Schools are co-educational and free. Most children go to their local school and mix with their neighbours, though there are a few private schools. Some provinces also have separate schools operated by Catholics or Protestants. Occasionally this has become a political issue, and Quebec's "Quiet Revolution" of the 1960s separated public education from the church. Today the schools in Quebec are French or English, Catholic or Protestant, but there remains some controversy over the language of instruction in all of them.

Universities: from revolution to resignation

Many students continue their education beyond high school and a degree or diploma is becoming a necessity in an increasingly competitive society. Ironically, many graduates are considered over-qualified by today's employers. There are about 60 universities, and over 365 schools which offer university-level courses. They tend to reflect a mixture of American and British influences. Some are small and social like Queen's, large city complexes like Toronto, ultra-modern like Simon Fraser, or French like Laval. Tuition fees are still affordable, and average about $500 a year; students work in the summer to pay their way, and also take out loans made available by the federal government. While many students live in halls of residence and co-operatives, it isn't unusual to live at home and commute. In general, the tightened economic situation has made students much more sedate, and university faculties are aware of the need to hire Canadian staff.

The taxpayer is also demanding his share of education and community colleges have filled this need. Adult education is on the increase. A unique example is Frontier College, established in 1900. Education no longer ends at graduation, but is becoming a life-long pleasure and preoccupation.

▲ Classroom atmosphere is relaxed, and as the posters for 1975's International Womens' Year shows, girls are encouraged to excel.

▼ Provincial governments encourage employers to hire students during the summer so that they can help support themselves. Even high schoolers take part-time jobs during the year.

Cet été, place aux jeunes!
Have a young Summer...
Embauchez des étudiants
Hire a Student

The Canadian school system

Nursery school 3-4

Secondary or High School—up to 18
4 or 5 grades, depending on the province

Institute of Technology or Community College

University
3 years B.A

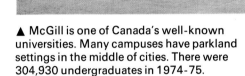

▲ McGill is one of Canada's well-known universities. Many campuses have parkland settings in the middle of cities. There were 304,930 undergraduates in 1974-75.

▼ High schools have many extracurricular activities. Bands and drama productions are impressively unamateurish; local charities are often supported by them.

▲ Most public school children look forward to Friday afternoon art classes. The two-month summer vacation is also eagerly awaited, if not always by their parents.

▼ In 1975-76 $11,487·8 million was spent on education and in the previous year 5,559,100 children under 18 were enrolled in publicly controlled schools.

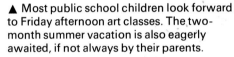

Kindergarten 4-5

Elementary school 6-13
7 or 8 grades, depending on the province

ars Honors

Post Graduate
MA 1 year, PhD 3 years

Artery to the heartland

The highway of New France

The St. Lawrence lured explorers to the heart of Canada and beyond. With settlement, it became the main highway for the boats and sleighs of New France, where every strip farm had its river frontage. The enterprising farmers, or *habitants*, rented land from the large land-owner, or *seigneur*, in the benevolently fuedalistic society of the seigniorial system. Many of the habitants beat the system by occasionally escaping into the interior to trade furs. The St. Lawrence provided easy access, and the swashbuckling *voyageurs* moved west following new supplies and contacts. In time, their canoes gave way to larger vessels. The Red River in modern Manitoba became a great food base, supporting the trading system as far as the Rockies.

The empire of the St. Lawrence

There was fierce trade rivalry, particularly between the river and the bay—between the North West Company and the Hudson Bay Company. The latter finally absorbed the Nor'Wester's in 1821. Although Montreal competed unsuccessfully with ice-free New York for the interior trade of North America, the vision of a commercial empire ruling that vast hinterland was not com-

▲ The first canal in Canada was built on the St. Lawrence in 1779, between the Lakes St. Louis and St. Francis. In remote areas today water transport is still important. Many canals were built in the early 1800's.

▲ The Rideau Canal, begun in 1826, allowed British gunboats access to the Great Lakes while avoiding American fire.

▶ At Niagara, honeymooners can stare at each other as well as at the American and Canadian Falls, among the largest and most famous in the world.

pletely disappointed. The St. Lawrence River System grew, uniting Upper and Lower Canada, despite friction between economic interests and politicians. When the fur trade diminished, lumber and grain were forwarded to Europe, and British manufacturers gained in return—all via the St. Lawrence. Finally the North West itself was won back with the railways, settlements and economic investment all made possible by that life-line of water.

Today, connecting canals, rivers and lakes form a waterway 2,280 miles long. Great tankers line the docks of Thunder Bay, and enormous quantities of wheat and iron ore move from railway cars to elevators to ships in an endless procession of prosperity. Montreal, the world's largest inland port, handles 18,000,000 tons of cargo a year.

In 1958, after 50 years of discussion and five years of construction, the St. Lawrence Seaway was finished, with five new locks built by Canada and two by the U.S. In 1972, Canada and the United States also signed an agreement to reverse the pollution of the lower Great Lakes. In a few years, even the sea lamprey, which attacks the lake trout, may be brought under control.

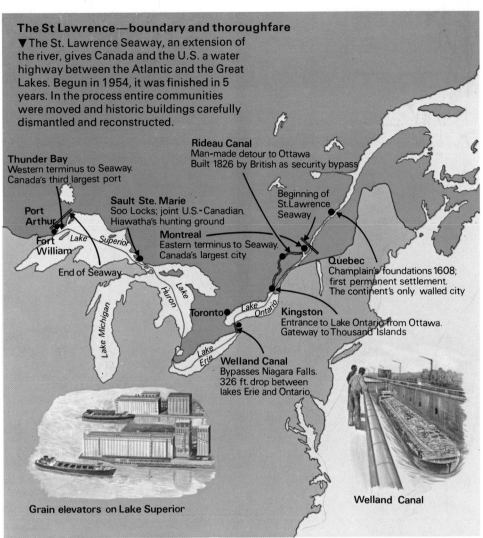

The St Lawrence—boundary and thoroughfare
▼ The St. Lawrence Seaway, an extension of the river, gives Canada and the U.S. a water highway between the Atlantic and the Great Lakes. Begun in 1954, it was finished in 5 years. In the process entire communities were moved and historic buildings carefully dismantled and reconstructed.

Thunder Bay
Western terminus to Seaway. Canada's third largest port

Port Arthur
Fort William

Rideau Canal
Man-made detour to Ottawa Built 1826 by British as security bypass

Sault Ste. Marie
Soo Locks; joint U.S.-Canadian. Hiawatha's hunting ground

Beginning of St. Lawrence Seaway

Montreal
Eastern terminus to Seaway. Canada's largest city

End of Seaway

Quebec
Champlain's foundations 1608; first permanent settlement. The continent's only walled city

Toronto

Kingston
Entrance to Lake Ontario from Ottawa. Gateway to Thousand Islands

Welland Canal
Bypasses Niagara Falls. 326 ft. drop between lakes Erie and Ontario

Grain elevators on Lake Superior

Welland Canal

▲ A barge at Montreal avoids rapids on the south side of the St. Lawrence by means of the Lachine Canal. The site of Expo '67 is just beyond and the "Man and his World" exhibit may still be seen there.

► The shortest international bridge in the world lies in the Thousand Islands, a beautiful Ontario resort area. The Canada-U.S. border is a friendly one and boat cruises attract many visitors.

From the Heights of Abraham

Mackenzie and his trail

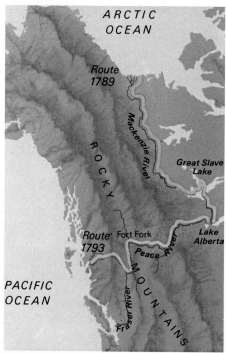

ARCTIC OCEAN

Route 1789

Mackenzie River

ROCKY

Great Slave Lake

Route 1793   Fort Fork   Lake Alberta

Peace River

PACIFIC OCEAN

MOUNTAINS

Fraser River

▲ The Scottish Alexander Mackenzie joined a Montreal fur-trading firm at 15. Ten years later in 1789, he travelled down the Mackenzie River to the Arctic Ocean, and in 1798 blazed a trail through the Rockies to the Pacific.

▶ Giant totem poles in Vancouver's Stanley Park and elsewhere were carved from cedar trees and were associated with the family histories of Pacific Coast Indians. The practice only really began in the last century.

Wars, treaties and visions

The growth of Canada from colony to nation began in 1759, during the Seven Years War. Britain gained New France with the Treaty of Paris in 1763, yet British governors proved generally sympathetic to the French. When the Americans attacked during their revolution against Britain, they were driven out by Governor Carleton and received surprisingly little local support. In the wake of the revolution came the United Empire Loyalists, 40,000 American immigrants loyal to the crown, whose 3,500,000 Canadian descendants today remember them with pride.

Canada continued British and loyal. When the war of 1812 between Britain and the U.S. erupted in Canada, she once again repelled the invasion and the war ended in stalemate. The Treaty of Ghent (1814) left French and British Canada more united, more attached to Britain, and more anti-American.

The Constitutional Act of 1791 had divided Quebec into Upper and Lower Canada. When Lord Durham was sent to Canada in 1838 to settle the rebellions led by Papineau and Mackenzie, he advised self-government and the separation of local and imperial concerns. Finding "two nations warring in the bosom of a single state", he also advised the union of the two regions. His brilliant report made some enemies, but it also began a new age for the entire British Empire.

▲ The interior of this Quebec home has been restored. Life in New France was sociable, if paternalistic and devoutly Catholic. Governors, Intendants and Bishops were the chief officials; among the most important were Frontenac, Talon and Laval.

◄ General Wolfe, and Montcalm, the able French commander, both died in the famous British victory on the Plains of Abraham in 1759. Quebec City was protected by strong defences on one side, steep cliffs on the other. After three frustrating months, Wolfe's men climbed the cliffs and surprised the French. With the Peace of Paris France lost her North American Empire, keeping only two small fishing islands.

▲ *Evangeline,* by the American poet, Longfellow, is the sad but romantic tale of an Acadian girl's search for her banished fiancée. Many French were expelled from Nova Scotia in the 1750s for refusing to swear allegiance to the British crown.

◄ The immigration of American loyalists helped to make Canada into a predominately English-speaking country.

Compromise and Confederation

A union formed in haste

The Union of Upper and Lower Canada proved unworkable, but Lord Durham's recommendations had done their work. Fear of U.S. conquest in the West, the interest in a railway system to foster trade, and common allegiance to Britain all contributed to the idea of a federal union. The British North America Act of 1867 established the Dominion of Canada. It included Nova Scotia, New Brunswick, Quebec and Ontario. Thus the foundations of the nation were laid peacefully; by compromise, conversation and loyalty to the British Crown.

By 1873, Canada would include the North West, British Columbia and Prince Edward Island. Although the North West Mounted Police prepared the western frontier for settlement, Canada's expansion was not without trouble. The Métis of the Red River settlement, European-Indian half breeds, felt that their way of life would be threatened. There were two ill-fated rebellions led by the unstable and tragic figure of Louis Riel. Manitoba was finally conquered and in 1871, with the Gold Rush behind it, British Columbia joined, spurred on by the promise of a railway and the efforts of Amor de Cosmos—whose real name was Smith!

The national dream

The Dominion had taken only four years to stretch from sea to sea. The Northwest Territories received responsible government in 1897; Alberta and Saskatchewan joined in 1905. With the discovery of Klondike gold fields on the Yukon River and the gold-rush of 1898-1903, the Yukon became a separate territory. Sir John A. Macdonald's Conservative National Policy attempted to fill in the outlines of a nation with a protective tariff, settlement and railways. The growth of the Canadian Pacific Railway is a dramatic chapter in the nation's history, filled with political manoeuvres, high costs and staggering geographical obstacles. Laurier, Canada's first French-Canadian Prime Minister, eventually supported Sir John A.'s policy, but advocated provincial rights. One Prime Minister created a nation; the other tried to bring its people together.

▲ The Fathers of Confederation— Macdonald, Galt, Tilley and Tupper, Cartier, Brown and McGee—meet for talks. Canadians persuaded Maritimers at the 1864 Charlottetown Conference to attend the Quebec Conference to discuss a larger union. Britain encouraged the idea, hoping it would strengthen Canada's defences. The London Conferences accepted the Quebec Resolutions, and the Dominion of Canada was born in 1867.

▼ Sir John A. Macdonald, the Father of Confederation, was the first Prime Minister of Canada. A wily and charming Conservative politician, he appealed to Canada's nationalism, anti-Americanism and loyalty to Britain in an attempt to establish Canada as a nation and to thwart free trade with the U.S.

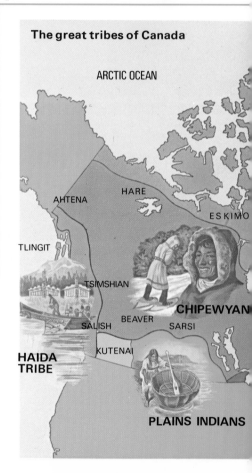

The great tribes of Canada

ARCTIC OCEAN

AHTENA

HARE

ESKIMO

TLINGIT

TSIMSHIAN

CHIPEWYAN

SALISH
BEAVER
SARSI

HAIDA
TRIBE

KUTENAI

PLAINS INDIANS

The Indians of Canada played a historic role in the development of the nation, both as allies of the colonizing French and English, and later as peacable victims of progress. Tecumseh and Joseph Brant were both famous chiefs. Tecumseh died in 1813, in the British defeat of Moraviantown, holding the rank of Brigadier-General in the War of 1812. A Shawnee chief, he had allied himself to the

▼ Louis Riel was the tragic, unbalanced and still controversial leader of two Metis uprisings. He set up his own provisional government, hoping to win better terms from Canada. But his execution of an English-speaking Canadian went too far. He fled to the U.S. and was later tried and hanged after the North West Rebellion.

▲ The hope of railways had stimulated Confederation. The Canadian Pacific was the most vital to national unity and the establishment of an East-West trading system. It took five years to build, half the contracted time. The last spike was driven at Craigallachie, British Columbia in 1885. The first CP train left Montreal in 1886; Lady Macdonald rode on the cowcatcher for the last 600 miles.

▼ In 1858 gold was discovered in the Fraser River. 30,000 miners rushed to the territory, and the British government formed the new colony of British Columbia. In 1896 gold was also discovered in the Klondike, and the rush began again. Dawson, below, grew to be a city of 25,000. Robert W. Service, the "poet of the Yukon", immortalized the "men who moiled for gold".

British in an unsuccessful attempt to organize a confederacy of tribes from Canada to Florida. Joseph Brant died in 1807; he formed the first Indian reserve in Canada in 1784. After fighting for the British in the American Revolution, he was granted 700,000 acres near today's Brantford, Ontario. Today, one-third of Canada's 270,000 Indians live on 23,775 sq. km. (9215 sq. mi.) of federal reserve.

Consolidation and Commonwealth

A parliamentary system

The BNA Act of 1867 was designed to combine the best features of British and American government. Canadian government has been stable and reflects all shades of opinion. The major parties, the Liberals and Progressive Conservatives, seem virtually indistinguishable—a Canadian phenomenon! Smaller parties like the New Democratic Party have occasionally held the balance of power in minority governments. The NDP offers its own brand of Canadian socialism; but then, Canadian history has always been a curious mixture of private enterprise and government support.

Unfortunately, Canadian politics have often been bedevilled by sectional tensions. French and English Canada have been divided over issues as far back as Louis Riel and the Conscription Crisis of World War I. Strong provincial governments try to extract as much power as possible from Ottawa. The Progressive Conservatives have dominated Ontario politics for over 32 years, the longest record in the western world. Quebec's return of a Liberal rather than separatist government suggests that that province will continue to put practicality before sentiment. There have been NDP premiers in B.C., Saskatchewan and Manitoba. The Liberal Prime Minister, Pierre Trudeau, however, has been a strong force in the ranks of the federalists.

▲ Macpherson's cartoons in the Toronto Star are famous for their shrewd observations. Canadians often seem like a squabbling family with different interests and temperaments.

▼ Queen Elizabeth II arrives in Toronto in 1973. Although less conspicuous than in the past, the crown adds a touch of glamour and patriotic sentiment to historic occasions.

▲ Queen Victoria chose Ottawa as Canada's federal capital. The gothic-style buildings were erected in the 1860s. Canada's government is among the world's most stable.

▲ Chairman Mao greets Pierre Trudeau, October 13, 1973. Canada has earned a place in diplomatic history as a peace-maker and builder of bridges. Prime Minister Trudeau's visit to Peking emphasized the innovative nature of Canada's foreign policy, since she had been the first Western country to recognize China, in 1970. Further agreements involved medical and educational exchanges.

▼ The Queen acts only in a symbolic and ceremonial capacity at the government's request, but there were demonstrations in Quebec during her last visit. Demonstrations also greeted De Gaulle, whose unwarranted "Vive Quebec libre" made the headlines. Good manners and good sense usually prevail in Canada, though some regional questions remain open.

▼ British Columbia's parliament buildings are in the delightfully English capital, Victoria. All provincial capitals boast impressive architecture.

A consumer society

Charge it!

Canadians love to shop. It is one of their favourite indoor sports. Since Canada is affluent, people tend to indulge themselves with their many credit cards. Most shops are open six days a week, but a few are even trying to stay open on Sundays and holidays. Service is generally good, though many shops are self-service to cut costs.

From supermarkets to fruit stands

One can go to the small neighbourhood shops or the local shopping centre—a large open air complex with many stores and a car park. Indoor shopping malls all under one roof are becoming increasingly popular too; like vast commercial cathedrals with fountains and escalators, they remain comfortable no matter what the temperature outside. A few years ago, shopping pilgrimages usually took one downtown. Today these large suburban centres with their department stores and boutiques keep people closer to home.

For a bit more local colour and cheaper prices, there is always a central open air market. Ethnic neighbourhoods also have their own speciality shops. In summer road stands tempt the traveller with everything from bait to blueberries. One can buy almost anything in Canada. For those who live in an isolated area, mail order catalogues are very convenient and still function as a guide to city fashions.

▲ Shopping malls provide entertainment for the entire family. But beware—getting everyone out is another matter!

▼ Although smaller specialty shops selling everything from cheese to coffee have faithful followings, large supermarkets are everywhere and are highly competitive.

▲ Canada's decimal system was adopted in 1858. The Canadian dollar has floated since 1970. Coins seem to have become smaller and silver rarer; officially they are 5, 10, 25 and 50 cent pieces. Unofficially, the American terms—nickels, dimes and quarters—prevail. The largest denomination of "bill" is the $1,000 note—not often encountered in day-to-day transactions!

▼ A woman buys flowers from the Kingston Market. The Kitchener Market in Ontario is also popular, with its picturesque Mennonite farmers. Local colour and prices both attract customers.

▲ Chips—or French fries—anyone? The sign is in *joual,* a French Canadian *franglais* which is often amusing. The ice cream man and his van provide another portable treat.

▲ From the 1880s onward, Eaton's catalogue gave remote areas outside links and stopped local overcharging. Best sellers seemed to be bibles and corsets with unbreakable ribs.

▶ Apples and pumpkins are sold at one of many roadside stands in the fall. They are favourite stops for summer travellers in fruit-growing areas.

Eating the Canadian way

Bon appetit!

Canadians are hearty eaters. Sometimes they overdo it. Every child grows up instilled with the ideals of good nutrition, enshrined in "Canada's Food Rules". But the reliance on cars rather than feet has made the fight against flab an uphill battle. Today's businessmen jog through their lunch hours at the local YMCA and health-conscious citizens have taken up cereals and cycling with equal passion.

When they are not counting calories or worrying about heart disease, Canadians have much to choose from on their food shelves. While taking full advantage of modern frozen foods, they are loyal to local specialities, from eastern clam chowders to *habitant* pea soups. Mme. Benoit is a national celebrity, famous for her French-Canadian recipes. The increase in immigration has also given Canadian food a cosmopolitan flavour. Caribbean and Asian products are more readily available, and household menus reflect family backgrounds from Japanese to Ukranian. German delicatessens are everywhere. Chinese and Italian restaurants flourish with their delivery service; the "Pizza Man" is a regular on college campuses.

Canadians generally eat at home, but for a family treat they often go to a pancake or steak house. Barbequed steak, hamburgers, hot dogs, corn-on-the-cob and salad are favourites, as they are in the U.S.

Commuting from suburb to city has meant briefer breakfasts and lighter lunches, with evening dinner the main meal of the day. But country life still promises a feast at every sitting.

Prost!

Tea, coffee, milk and soft drinks are the usual accompaniments to meals, though Canadians are proud of their domestic wine industry, based in the sheltered Niagara Peninsula and in British Columbia. The German Oktoberfest with its enthusiastic beer drinking has been happily adopted by Canadians; nevertheless, only government stores may sell spirits, and strict local drinking laws often amuse more liberal European visitors.

Make a Canadian meal

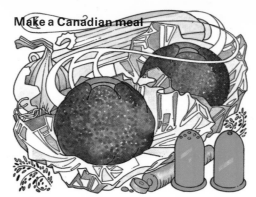

▲ Buffalo Birds

This is a recipe from Fort Smith in the Northwest Territories. If there are no buffalos around, try minced beef!

Heat the oven to 375 F. (Gas 5). Mix together 1 lb. ground buffalo meat or minced steak; 1 tsp. salt, 1 tsp. pepper and 1 egg.

Pat into four large patties on a floured board. Then combine 1 cup fine dry bread-crumbs; ½ cup chopped celery; 1 diced onion; ½ cup grated carrot; ½ tsp. sage and 1 egg.

Place a mound of this stuffing on each patty and form the meat around it. Wrap each ball in foil and bake at above heat for 45 min. Open foil and bake another 15 min. Serve.

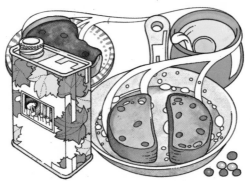

▼ Maritime Baked Beans

Put 1¾ lb. brown beans in a large saucepan. Pour in enough water to cover by 2 in. Bring to boil for 2 min., then let beans soak for an hour. Bring to boil again and add 1 whole peeled onion and 1 tsp. salt. Half cover and simmer for 30 min. Discard water and onion.

Preheat oven to 250 F. (Gas 2) and put the beans into a heavy casserole on top of two onions, peeled and studded with 2 cloves each. In a bowl, combine 6 tbs. molasses, 6 oz. brown sugar, 2 tsp. mustard and 1 tsp. each of salt and pepper. Stirring slowly, add ¾ pint of water. Pour this mixture over the beans, and add ½ lb. salt pork. Cover and bake in oven for 5 hrs. Remove cover, sprinkle with 2 oz. brown sugar, bake ½ hr. longer.
Serve.

◄ Anisk-Nah Be Pakwejigan (Real Indian Bread)

Bring to boil 1¾ cups of water. In a bowl mix together ⅔ cup of white corn flour (from health shops) and ¾ tsp. salt. Pour boiling water on dry ingredients while stirring until mix is thick. Stir in ½ cup blueberries or raisins and then chill until set. When firm, cut into slices and fry in butter. Serve with butter or maple syrup.

Regional menus

British Columbia
Crabmeat pastries
Fraser River salmon
Scalloped tomatoes
Capitano rye bread
Trifle
To drink: Okanagan apple juice

Quebec
Onion soup with cheese
Tourtiere (Quebec pork pie)
Ratatouille (onions, peppers, tomatoes)
French bread
Maple fudge
To drink: homemade wine

▼ A waitress serves a typical meal in a western restaurant where appetites match the hospitality. Service and quality are usually excellent. There is a wide variety of restaurants and Montreal claims title to the gastronomic capital of North America.

▲ A woman smokes fish. Some of the best food fishes in the world come from Canada's northern waters. About 16,000 Canadians work in fish processing plants. Salmon is the most valuable species on the Pacific coast and lobster on the Atlantic. Cod, which first attracted fishermen, can be 6' long.

▶ Maple syrup has always been associated with Canada and occurs in many recipes. It was traded in Quebec as early as 1685. Originally Indians nicked trees with their tomahawks, caught the sap in birchbark containers and then boiled it in earthen pots. It still makes a delicious treat on snow during winter outings and adds flavour to anything from candy to cocktails.

Ontario
Hot cheese tartlets
Honey chicken with rhubarb relish
Steamed wild rice
Turnips and apples
Butternut spice cake
To drink: Ontario white wine

Maritime Provinces
P.E.I. potato soup
Corned beef and cabbage
Bread and butter pickles
Corn fritters
Molasses tarts
To drink: Newfoundland blueberry wine

Prairie Provinces
Winnipeg goldeye trout
Salt-broiled steak
Yorkton Nachynka (Ukrainian stuffing)
Dandelion salad
Alberta honey-apple pie
To drink: Canadian beer

Big sportsmen and the great outdoors

The game and the gear

▲ Lacrosse is a Canadian game played by two sets of twelve. The ball is driven through the opponents' goal by a *crosse*, a long stick with a shallow net at one end. Indians called it baggataway and 200 could play. The Iroquois used it to train warriors, and it is still a rough-and-tumble sport. Newsy Lalonde was one of the greatest players of the last half-century—he was also an outstanding hockey player.

"He shoots, he scores!"

Canadians enjoy spectator sports. Occasionally they can even be persuaded to join in themselves. Golf, tennis, skating, bridge, skiing and curling are favourite pastimes. They are avid fans of American-style football, and baseball too is a popular children's sport, as well as a professional league one. But ice hockey is the great passion and Canada's game. The first Russia-Canada professional series in 1972 aroused incredible patriotic fervour; after a poor start, Canada won. Hockey may well have originated on Christmas Day, 1885, when soldiers cleared the snow from the harbour, put on skates and used field hockey sticks with a lacrosse ball.

Lacrosse is Canada's oldest and roughest game, invented by the Indians. Canadians also invented basketball and 5-pin bowling. Canada has a Sports Hall of Fame and is proud of her successes. The schooner *Blue-nose* is particularly close to the heart of Maritimers; launched in 1921, she won the sailing championship of the fishing fleets of the North Atlantic and never lost the trophy.

In the 1972 Munich Olympic Games Canadians won two silver and three bronze medals and in March of that year Karen Magnussen won the world figure skating title. Once Canadians themselves leave their cities, they enjoy the great outdoors wholeheartedly. Going "up north" is part of the Canadian tradition and rhythm, whether it means going fifty miles or a thousand.

▲ Yvon Cournoyer and Murray Wilson play hockey against the California Golden Seals at the Montreal Forum. Ice hockey is fast, furious and exciting. Old buffs complain that rapid expansion into American cities has lowered standards and increased violence. Russian competition should improve that!

▼ Queen's University plays football, a very popular school, college and professional sport in the autumn. Canadian football differs slightly from the American version.

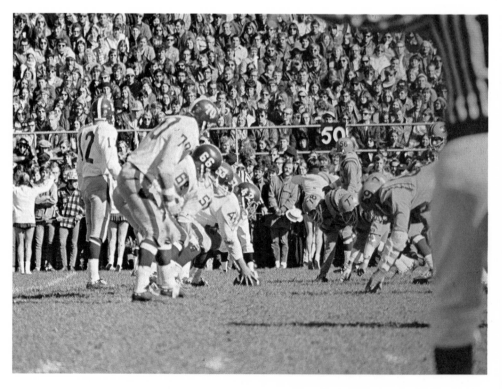

▼ Fish stories are true in Canada! Ice fishing huts are familiar winter sights on frozen lakes. The autumn smelt run up the St. Lawrence is a less solitary occasion.

▲ Climbing on Mt. Robson is exhilarating— and what a view! Canadians have excelled at skiing too, and Nancy Greene is a particularly well-known medalist. Snowshoeing affords a good way of seeing the country for the less daring.

▼ Strike three and you're out! Young men and boys find baseball especially fun. Businesses often sponsor local teams and many companies have their own.

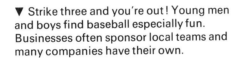

▲ Boys bring home rabbits for the pot. Not an unusual sight, particularly on the prairies. Wildlife is carefully regulated, but Canada is still a paradise for hunters.

A natural talent

Popular culture

The arts have prospered in the last few decades. There are many fine museums and art galleries in Canada. The Royal Ontario Museum in Toronto is the country's largest, and is famous for its extensive Chinese collection. The $46 million National Arts Centre which seats 2,300 opened in Ottawa in 1969 and hosts many touring companies.

Elsewhere theatre is also growing and the Dominion Drama Festival is an annual competition for amateur groups. The National Theatre School has courses in English and French in Stratford, Ontario, world-famous for its Shakespeare productions. Music and drama festivals are popular events and eagerly awaited. They are held every year at Montreal, Vancouver, Niagara-on-the-Lake, and Guelph, Ontario. There are also six professional symphony orchestras, as well as a National Youth orchestra and three leading opera companies. Winnipeg, Toronto and Quebec have three professional ballet companies of international status. The choice of films is wide and the National Film Board has received world acclaim for its productions. Culture lives in Canada!

Art at home—and abroad

Canada is not short of talent and there has been a great art boom. Canadians write operas on Louis Riel as well as long dramas on Hitler. Northrop Frye influenced a whole generation of "small fry" with his brand of literary criticism, which is equally at home with European classics and the Canadian imagination. French-Canadian *chansonniers* like Gilles Vigneault have devoted followings at home and at international festivals. Canada's art and culture are becoming distinctively her own, while achieving universal appeal and professional excellence. The land imposes its own perception on its people. Emily Carr and the Group of Seven have painted it with bold, original strokes. Karsh has photographed its faces.

▶ *Sled and Cutter on the Ice of the St. Lawrence,* painted by Cornelius Krieghof in 1861. His paintings of Quebec *habitants,* Indians and winter scenes are highly-prized at home and abroad.

▲ Aopilardjuk Mariano (b. 1923) is perhaps Canada's best-known Eskimo carver. The practical Eskimos were not always deliberate artists, but their soapstone sculptures and stone-cut prints are now avidly collected.

▶ A character study of Canada's well-loved humorist, Stephen Leacock, taken by the internationally-famous photographer, Karsh. Leacock's amusing *Sunshine Sketches of a Little Town* is a North American classic.

▲ *Henry IV* is presented at the Stratford Shakespeare Festival in Ontario. Performances are in an Elizabethan theatre-in-the-round, though the plays are not always period.

▲ *Pine-Cleft Rocks,* painted by Tom Thomson in 1915 in Algonquin Park. He died there mysteriously in 1917, after a brief but brilliant career. *The Group of Seven* has dominated Canadian painting with its bold, vivid approach to landscape.

▶ The mad scene in Act I of the ballet *Giselle.* Winnipeg, Toronto and Quebec all have professional ballet companies, and seeing the *Nutcracker Suite* is something of a Christmas ritual.

▼ *Anne of Green Gables* by Lucy Maude Montgomery, a celebrated children's book, has been filmed and dramatized numerous times.

The ethnic enterprise

Where the immigrants settled

▼ Heavy immigration has coincided with the American Revolution, the Irish famine, and the opening of the West. Three million settlers came between 1900 and 1914. Post-war immigration has made Canada even more cosmopolitan.

The immigrant and the native

Canada is more of a mosaic than a melting pot. Although French Canada has a culture of its own, the two founding peoples of French and British stock are not alone; the next largest ethnic groups are the Germans, followed by the Ukranians, Italians, and people from the Netherlands, Scandinavia and Poland. Since World War II Canada has offered a new life to more than 3 million people, from as far away as Chile and Tibet. The first census of Canada taken in 1666 showed 3,215 white inhabitants. Today there are over 22 million. The result is an interesting and sophisticated country whose lack of homogeneity ensures much individual freedom, if not a characteristic national identity. Canadians are a tolerant and generous people who respect fellow citizens as long as they mow their front lawn.

Modern life has not always been as kind to the Indian, as the high infant mortality rate and lower life expectancy suggest. It was not until 1960 that the right to vote was given to 60,000 Indians on reservations. The recent upsurge of interest in their own culture and land rights, particularly near Hudson's Bay, indicate that the first Canadians are making themselves heard.

◄ An Eskimo woman plays cat's cradle, a game Canadian children also enjoy. Eskimos had no written language until missionaries devised a system of signs at the end of the last century. Canada now has 15,000 Eskimos.

▼ An Indian woman celebrates the Calgary stampede. Indians have been called Canada's most economically depressed group, and they are actively bargaining for property rights. The Lieutenant Governor of Alberta is an Indian, the first appointed in Canada.

▲ A Ukrainian family celebrates their "second" Christmas. In some Manitoba areas, the Julian calendar is still observed, and Ukrainian churches with their onion domes are familiar sights. There is an annual Ukrainian Festival in Dauphin and a yearly Icelandic gathering in Gimli, Manitoba.

▼ A Japanese woman fillets fish. Many Japanese came to British Columbia, and their detention in camps during World War II aroused much controversy. A Japanese Friendship Garden in the traditional style, as well as the second largest Chinatown in North America, are both in Vancouver.

▲ A group of German marchers in Vancouver's Dominion Day Parade The largest group after the French and the British, the Germans settled mainly in the West and in Ontario.

Language and communication

Leaders in telecommunications

Without a wide-ranging communication system Canada would not survive. Telecommunications tie the country together and the Federal Government is anxious to retain control despite provincial pressures. In 1969 a Department of Communications was established as well as Telesat; Anik, Eskimo for brother, is a satellite which provides communications link to the remotest regions. In April 1973 Anik II was launched, and in May 1975 a third satellite was sent up. A fourth, even more powerful, was planned for 1976. Canada stole a march on the U.S. with the world's first nationwide digital data network, which is reliable and faster than normal telephone networks.

The telephone is an indispensible fact of life to most Canadians. It was invented in Brantford, Ontario, by Alexander Graham Bell in 1874. Today 96% of all homes have one and Canadians are addicted to talking on the phone. Fortunately costs are low and local calls are free. When Canadians are not on the phone, they may be watching television; 97% of Canadian homes have one. There are 60 privately owned TV stations and 270 privately owned radio stations. The CBC offers wide services, however, broadcasting in French and English and providing a special radio service to the northern territories. About 80% of Canadians have access to cable T.V., which has much potential.

Bilingualism and biculturalism

Two-thirds of Canadians speak only English. About one-third speak mainly French and 12% speak both. Less than 2% speak neither. It is official policy in the civil service to be bilingual. Although there are some regional accents most notably in the Maritimes, it is generally difficult to tell where a Canadian comes from. French is mostly spoken in Quebec and English outside, with the exception of a few areas in New Brunswick and the Prairies. With the controversial passing of Bill 22 in Quebec, teaching in French has been encouraged—much to the displeasure of the Italian community there.

▲ Alexander Graham Bell invented the telephone in his father's Brantford, Ontario, house in 1874. But many later inventions were completed in the U.S.

▼ There are over 800 weekly newspapers, 750 business magazines, 350 consumer magazines and 50 farm papers. American magazines using Canada as a tax haven have caused much controversy.

▲ The owner of this lone mailbox on the prairie looks forward to news of the outside world. Even remote areas often receive regular services; but the post office is still a community centre in small villages.

▼ Despite sore feet and long treks, the mail must go through. But services seem to be decreasing with increasing costs, and Canadians are often frustrated by long mail strikes.

▲ *Bilangue et Biculte.* Aside from the Civil Service, B & B has not been a complete success. But there are many bilingual signs and most labels are in two languages

▼ Canadian place names reflect Indian words, the origins of the inhabitants and their adventures. Cartier gave Canada her name—from the Indian "Kannata", meaning a collection of huts.

A television selection

Television runs a long day, from 6 a.m. to 3 a.m. next day. The Canadian Broadcasting Corp. and commercial TV stations share some 20 channels. There is growing concern over the large number of American programmes dominating the Canadian small screen. Situation comedies and police thrillers are popular. The following shows 2 hours' viewing on a Tuesday evening:

8.00 p.m.
(2) (8) Movin' On
(4) NBA Basketball
(5) (3) (7) (8) (10) (12) (13) Happy Days
(6) (22) WHA Hockey
(9) (10) (13) Good Times
(11) Cannon
(17) Last of the Mohicans
(19) The Disappearing World
(25) La P'tite Semain
(29) Star Trek
(79) Money Game
9.00 p.m.
(2) (8) Police Woman
(5) (3) (8) (10) (12) The Fifth Estate
(7) (9) (13) The Rookies
(10) M*A*S*H
(11) Barbetta
(17) The Ascent of Man
(19) Masters in their own Houses
(25) Rue des Pignons

▶ Moose Jaw, Saskatchewan, probably comes from the Indian word meaning "river that bends like a mooses jaw". But legend suggests a pioneer mended his oxcart wheel there with a jawbone.

▲ Flin Flon, Manitoba, was named after Josiah Flintabbatey Flonatin, a character in a dime novel much read by local prospectors with little else to choose from. Later the novel, *The Sunless City,* was tracked down in London.

▼ Saskatoon, Saskatchewan, "Potash Capital of the World" is named after a bush with purple berries, regarded as a delicacy by the Indians.

41

The Canadian achievement

Forestry

- Cobalt
- Iron
- Uranium
- Gold
- Lead
- Silver
- Copper
- Potassium
- Nickel
- Asbestos
- Platinum
- Lithium
- Vanadium

Canada's wealth: minerals and timber

▲ Canada leads the world in the production of asbestos, nickel, silver and zinc. Coal along the Atlantic, and bog-iron ore in Quebec were the initial discoveries, and today mining leads all industry in export value.

▼ A hydro-electric dam in the St. Lawrence Seaway is beautified by the French Fleur-de-Lis. Canada is second only to the U.S. in the harnessing of water power, and both share the enormous resources of the Great Lakes.

The energy crisis

World shortages have forced Canada to appreciate her great natural treasures. Much is exchanged with the U.S.—coal, electricity, uranium, natural gas and water. With increased modern demand, public concern has often made such decisions controversial and Canada is phasing out oil and gas exports to the U.S. In the next ten years Arctic gas, or oil extracted from the Athabaska tar sands may be forthcoming, although the latter is a particularly difficult operation. A pipeline to transport this oil through Canada, rather than Alaska, has also been the subject of hot debate.

Canada ranks about ninth in world petroleum production, and twelfth in reserves. One of the world's longest pipeline systems moves more than 600,000,000 barrels a year 2,023 miles from Alberta to Ontario. Second

▲ This is the Rio Alto Ranch in Alberta. Cattle ranching is popular in the West where ranches like Stetsons come big; one covers 2.5 million acres. The parks and foothills of southwest Alberta are particularly suited to livestock, and meat-packing was another early source of provincial prosperity.

in the world's per capita production of electricity, she counts water power as one of her greatest resources. While the world's largest power plant is under construction at Churchill Falls, Labrador, the first U.S. nuclear station on Lake Huron operates on the method pioneered in Canada, which uses uranium and heavy water.

Agriculture is Canada's second most important industry and wheat is produced in the greatest quantity. Her forests cover 3 million square kilometres (1.2 million square miles), and there are about 150 native varieties of trees. Half of the newspaper pages in the western world are printed on Canadian paper. Her fisheries are the most important in the world; a keen conservationist, she hopes to persuade foreign fishermen to reduce their catch by 40% and to control a 200-mile zone off her coasts.

▲ Yellowknife was established as a gold-mining town. Its name comes from the Yellowknife Indians and their copper tools. The two large mines are the Consolidated and the Yellowknife.

◀ This is a Trans-Canada Pipeline Gas Compressor Station and the spheres, or "scrubbers", are cleaners.

▲ This is a sodium factory and natural sulphur deposit in Regina. Saskatchewan's mineral output has quadrupled in the last decade and there has been debate about the nationalization of potash.

◀ Timber floats down the Gatineau River. There are about one million square miles of productive forest, mostly on Crown lands.

Turbines and dog sleds

Bluenose seamen

The Maritimes had their shipbuilding heyday in the era of "wood, wind and water". Their clipper ships were superbly designed, and Nova Scotia seamen developed a leading merchant fleet. In 1833 the *Royal William*, built at Quebec, was the first vessel to cross the Atlantic under steam the entire way. Seven years later, Samuel Cunard of Halifax sent the first Cunard across.

Today ships carry a quarter of all freight. The St. Lawrence Seaway handles 45 million tons of cargo in a season. Once the *voyaguer* canoe skimmed the Lakes. Now noisy power boats disturb the tranquility of the northern lakes. So too do snowmobiles, the basis of a dangerous, if popular, sport. In the Arctic, however, they are particularly useful vehicles, and have replaced the patrol sleigh dogs of the Royal Canadian Mounted Police. In 1969 the last husky was retired, thus ending a 70-year-old tradition.

Today distance means little to Canadians. There are nearly 450,000 miles of well-maintained highway—a far cry from the bumpy log "corduroy" roads of Upper Canada. Canadians are not keen walkers, and they will take the car around the block. If people can't drive, they fly. There are two major airlines, government owned Air Canada, and privately owned Canadian Pacific. Similarly there are two rail systems —the privately owned Canadian Pacific and publicly owned Canadian National.

▲ Only horsedrawn vehicles called *calèches* are allowed on the top of Mont Royal, Montreal.

▼ Canada's fire-fighting planes (Canadair CL-215 amphibian) and her short take-off and landing planes for inter-city and northern flights are famous—particularly De Havilland Beavers and Otters.

◄ Railways are Canada's main means of transport. In the last decade 1500 miles of new railway line have been built. Computerization, piggy-back trains and containerization are all improving freight-handling.

▲ Only Toronto operates electric street cars as well as regular buses. Toronto also claims the country's oldest subway—built in 1954, it is 26 miles long. Intercity buses carry over 50 million passengers a year.

▼ Expressways and junctions such as this one in Don Valley, near Toronto, allow faster travelling and access to city centres. But government planners now question their long-term efficiency.

◄ Bridges are important in a land bisected by numerous channels and rivers. The tall, scenic Lion's Gate Bridge in Vancouver stretches from Stanley Park across the city's harbour.

▲ The Royal Canadian Mounted Police now use snowmobiles rather than the specially-trained Siberian huskies in the North. But some Eskimos and trappers still use the legendary dog-sled.

Customs and celebrations

▲ The Famous Winter Carnival in Quebec lasts for two weeks until Shrove Tuesday. It attracts thousands of visitors to its canoe races, dog derbies, *Bonspiel*, peewee hockey championships and convivial French-Canadian gatherings.

The best of many worlds

Canada's celebrations reflect the varied customs of her people, from Chinese New Year parades to Ukranian festivals in Manitoba. They also reflect a mixture of British and American influences, though Thanksgiving does not have the same importance and date as the American variety. There are nine public holidays and each province adds a few of its own, with the occasional fire cracker display thrown in for good measure. Quebec has a number of saints' days, like St. Catherine's Day with its toffee-pulling.

A celebration for every season

In the summer, country fairs abound. The Canadian National Exhibition in Toronto is the biggest of them all, mixing candy floss with culture, trade exhibits with midway rides. The Calgary Stampede, Buffalo Days at Regina and Klondike Days at Edmonton all prove exciting occasions for local people and tourists as the wild west springs to life. Christmas nights are lit up with good cheer and bright decorations on private homes and public buildings. New Year's Eve is an excuse for a night on the town. Winter is also enlivened with the famous Quebec Winter Carnival, its ice sculpture and sports. At Easter children all over await the Easter Rabbit with his candy eggs. Birthdays and anniversaries, weddings and showers for prospective brides and expectant mothers all demand some celebration, even if just cake and sandwiches.

▼ With football teams like the Ottawa Rough Riders, the Calgary Stampeders, Hamilton Tiger Cats and Winnipeg Bombers, no one expects Grey Cup finals to be tame events!

◀ Like most stampedes, the Falkland Stampede in British Columbia generates much excitement. The Calgary is the largest in the world, with hair-raising chuck wagon races, bronco and bull-busting, and a rodeo.

▲ Every October, children look forward to dressing up for their Hallowe'en rounds. Pumpkins become hollowed-out faces lit with candles greeting ghostly visitors. Cries of "trick or treat" ring through the suburbs.

▲ Near Whitehorse in the Yukon, an Indian graveyard has graves covered by miniature "Spirit Houses". They are intended to provide comfort and pleasure in the after-life of the dead.

▼ In July, Edmonton brings the gold rush to life with her Klondike Days. All kinds of races —bathtub, beer and raft—Klondike Kate, and a mine salted with real gold nuggets recapture the spirit of '98.

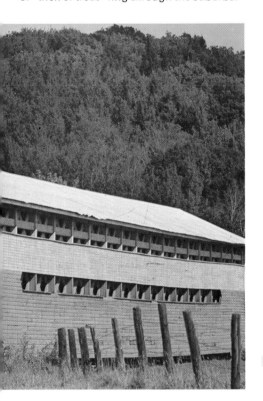

▲ "Kissing bridges" have roofs which act as snow guards. The world's longest covered bridge is in Hartland, New Brunswick—over 1,282 ft. There are more than 160 of these picturesque bridges in the province.

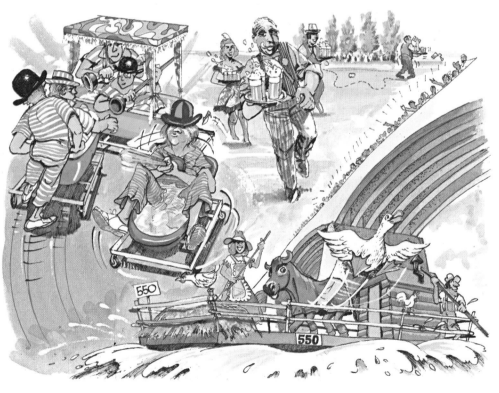

Heroes of flesh and blood

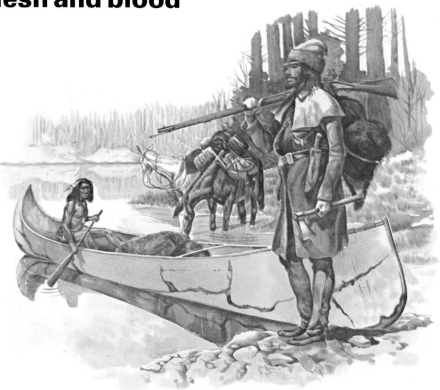

▲ Romantic *coureurs de bois* took to the woods and traded with the Indians. Some went native in the process. On the St. Lawrence, swashbuckling *voyageurs* often carried 180 pounds, surviving on salt pork, pemmican and strong tobacco.

▼ Canadian air aces and bush pilots are renowned. Billy Bishop, below, shot down 72 enemy aircraft in World War I. Northern bush pilots ferry supplies to distant outposts, and regularly save the lives of stranded hunters.

A Country without a Mythology?

The land has made many of its inhabitants heroic. Its early history is full of giants like Champlain and Frontenac. The *coureurs de bois* and the *voyageurs* have been romantic figures in modern times, if not always in their own, when many criticized their "libertinism" and tendency to go native.

The great Canadian hero can often be a tragic one. Brébeuf and his fellow priests were martyred. Montcalm and Wolfe both died on the Plains of Abraham. General Brock died at the Battle of Queenston Heights. The ill-fated rebel, Louis Riel, was hanged—and still arouses controversy. Yet history has given Canada her share of traditional heroes: Mounties and bush pilots, heroines like Laura Secord and Madeleine de Vercheres, inventors like Bell and Fleming, rebels like Papineau and Mackenzie, Indian chiefs like Tecumseh and Brant, hockey stars and pop singers, fathers of Confederation like Sir John A. Macdonald.

More recent Prime Ministers have had their share of adulation; John Diefenbaker ("Dief the Chief") attracted fierce devotion and opposition; Lester Pearson won a Nobel Prize and an international reputation.

But in general, hero worship embarrasses Canadians, who have little awe for living legends. They have had to struggle too hard themselves.

▲ Few honeymoon couples at Niagara Falls face Blondin's hazards. The mid-nineteenth century tightrope expert crossed the falls with a wheelbarrow, blindfolded, cooking an omelette, and with his manager piggy-back!

▼ William Lyon Mackenzie was Toronto's first mayor in 1835. Like Papineau in Lower Canada, he led an ill-starred rebellion against the ruling clique, later fleeing to the U.S. It is said he still haunts his Toronto home.

▲ The Mounties Musical Ride is a regular attraction. The 1874 Great March west established their fine reputation. In four rough months they covered 1,000 miles, routing whiskey traders without losing a single man.

▶ Lester "Mike" Pearson won an international reputation for diplomacy over the Suez Crisis, and was awarded the Nobel Peace Prize. John Diefenbaker, his predecessor, probably had more home support.

白求恩同志毫不利己专门利人的精神，表现在他对工作的极端的负责任，对同志对人民的极端的热忱。每个共产党员都要学习他。

毛泽东

▲ Dr. Norman Bethune is much respected in China, where he was a surgeon and attended Mao Tse-Tung. Deeply committed to the Chinese revolutionary cause, he died of blood poisoning while operating on wounded Communists. His Ontario birthplace was visited by China's championship ping-pong team in 1972.

The Canadian character

▶ The shotgun marriage between French and English-speaking Canada has become a marriage of convenience. Hopefully a divorce won't ensue.

▲ Trudeau has cut a dash, but other nations often think Canadian politics boring. Canadian complacency about their political purity abroad and security at home has led to the phrase "Ugly American, smugly Canadian."

A split personality

The "average" Canadian likes to be inconspicuous—unless mistaken for an American—but he will defend Americans to the British and vice versa. In short, the Canadians like peace. They don't make waves, and assume all's right with the world. If a minor scandal embarrasses the government, they feel faintly gratified to share notoriety with the major powers. They get the limelight all the time!

But Canadians really are a difficult breed to define. Regional attitudes are strong: Westerners and Maritimers growl at Easterners in prosperous central Canada; they in turn remain oblivious—except to retaliate with the odd regional joke. People in the North West Territories complain about the government's imperialism; northern Ontario folk mutter about "Hogtown" Toronto

▲ Innocents abroad. Canadians enjoy travelling, especially through olde-worlde Britain. Though unobtrusive in manner, they usually manage to put a maple leaf somewhere.

◀ Montreal Canadians return victorious after winning the National Hockey League's Stanley Cup. The Canadian love of ice hockey and a good time guarantees everyone a party when the team comes home.

and the south—unless, of course, they've already moved there themselves. Maritimers feel neglected, Westerners abused. There are English-Canadians who complain about expensive Gallic tastes, but civilized people are just tired of hyphenated Canadians. Everyone blames everyone else for their own problems — particularly American domination. Will the Great Canadian Identity Crisis ever be solved? Canada probably couldn't survive it.

Live and let live

Despite their differences, Canadians get along amicably enough—they are too polite to do otherwise. Canadian society is really a middle-class one: clean-living, conservative and hard-working, always materialistic and surprisingly cheerful. If Canadians ever seem a little smug with their enviable lot, they would be the first to apologize.

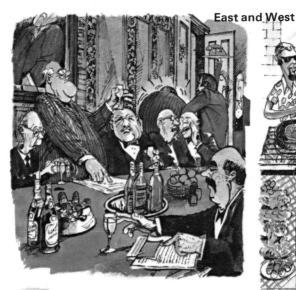

East and West

An easy-going nature

▲ Regional stereotypes exist even in business. The dark-suited tycoons of Toronto contrast sharply with "cool" western executives.

◀ Canadians tend to feel someone's minding the shop. Though they've had access to American know-how, British political wisdom and French culture, Canadians have managed to end up with British know-how, French political wisdom and American culture.

▲ Canada is often called "tomorrow" country. Young, optimistic, she shares with the U.S. a pride in a pioneer past. But this common bond cannot disguise fears for her identity.

▶ Canadians have a reputation for ruggedness and energy. They'll fight flab, but they've been spoiled. Affluent and sheltered, will they really begin to live today for tomorrow, and not just for itself?

The maple leaf forever?

Oh! Canada

Canadians have never really been great flag wavers. There have been many laments and ultimatums for this nation recently, but nationalism has never been more intense, especially among young people. Centennial celebrations in 1967 generated much enthusiasm. Today there is a great awareness of U.S. domination of Canadian industry, a development which has guaranteed a high standard of living, but at the cost of Canadian control. American cultural influence is also inescapable. Though their undefended border is justly world-famous, it has been said that Canada is like a mouse in bed with an elephant. No matter how kindly disposed the elephant, any movement is of vital concern to the mouse. Good fences make good neighbours.

It is unlikely that Canadians will sacrifice such affluence for economic independence. But it is even more unlikely that they will sacrifice their political independence. Canada's historical development, her institutions, her temperament, have always been different to those of the U.S. Today she is looking for a "third option", a special link with the EEC, which seems to be on the point of materializing, thanks to Trudeau's efforts. That Canada has so far overcome all the barriers to her survival suggests she will continue to do so. Canada has always seemed an impossible dream.

The True North, Strong and Free

Her land forces one to use superlatives; her British institutions give stability; her French presence makes her unique. To ensure their future, Canadians must look beyond the ledger and their provincial boundaries. French and English Canadians must realize they are each other's best allies; both must have greater confidence in Canadian enterprise. The government is already screening foreign take-overs. With all her resources, Canada may yet manage to claim her future as her own.

▲ New replaces old in Montreal, and walls crumble. FLQ terrorism and the 1970 October Kidnap Crisis underlined discontent with Quebec's social structure. Though the French-Canadian nationalists want more power, they may still manage to achieve it within the existing system.

▲ "I'm tired of being just another hewer of wood and drawer of water". —A comment on the Canadian dilemma. Canada's vast natural wealth has tended to obscure the importance of her manufacturing output—half of which is unrelated to primary resources. She ranks 6th in world volume of manufacturing, but further development rests largely with government attitudes and American investment.

▼ Getting the 1976 Olympics was quite a coup for Montreal's ingenious Mayor Drapeau, but many Canadians felt it was an expensive and unnecessary luxury. The delay in building and the escalating costs also caused much agonized debate. But the outstanding architecture and sporting thrills really put Canada on the map.

Olympiade XXI Olympiad Montréal 1976

Canada 50

▲ Demonstrators make their feelings felt outside the national parliament. By world standards Canada is a privileged society. Although her government depends on many unwritten rules, the law ensures equal opportunity.

▼ An artist works on a sculpture called "Pollution". Canadians are keen conservationists, and are particularly concerned about water resources and the lower Great Lakes. She hopes that the U.S. will live up to their agreement to clean up these natural reservoirs.

▼ Not everyone can have an aeroplane parked outside their front door, but many of the 19,700 Canadian civil aircraft are privately owned.

Reference
Human and physical geography

FACTS AND FIGURES
Position: North America, between Atlantic and Pacific Oceans; north of the United States of America.
Expanse: 3,223 miles, east to west 2,875 miles, north to south.
Area: 3.8 million square miles; second largest country in the world after Russia.
Capital: Ottawa, Ontario.
Political divisions: ten provinces, two territories.
Population: 22.7 million (1975).
Ethnic groups: British origin 40%; French origin 30%; native peoples 1.1%; Métis (French and Indian) 0·9%; the remainder primarily from European states.
Language: two official, English and French. 66% speak English only; 20% speak French only; 12% speak both.
Religions: largest denominations are Roman Catholic 45%; United Church of Canada 20%; Anglican Church of Canada 13%; Presbyterians 4%; Lutherans 3½%; Baptists 3%.

Climate

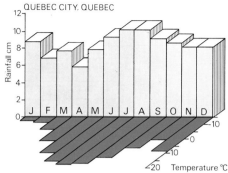
QUEBEC CITY, QUEBEC

Annual rainfall of Canada

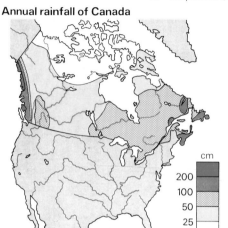

cm
200
100
50
25

Although Canada is a large country, one can generalize; winters are cold and summers warm. Spring tends to be short. Autumn is particularly colourful and pleasant, especially when a warm spell, or "Indian summer" occurs just before winter. The west coast has the highest precipitation; the Maritimes the heaviest snowfall. Droughts can occur on the prairies.

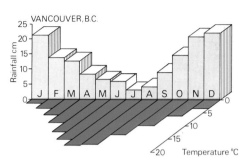
VANCOUVER, B.C.

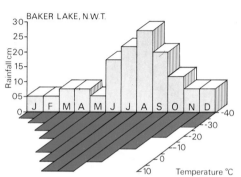
BAKER LAKE, N.W.T.

Canadian vegetation

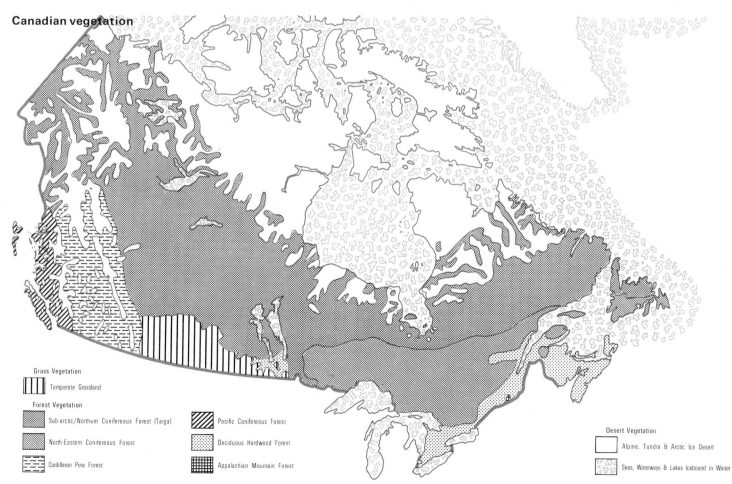

Grass Vegetation
- Temperate Grassland

Forest Vegetation
- Sub-arctic/Northern Conifereous Forest (Taiga)
- North-Eastern Conifereous Forest
- Cordilleran Pine Forest
- Pacific Conifereous Forest
- Deciduous Hardwood Forest
- Appalachian Mountain Forest

Desert Vegetation
- Alpine, Tundra & Arctic Ice Desert
- Seas, Waterways & Lakes Icebound in Winter

Population of principal cities

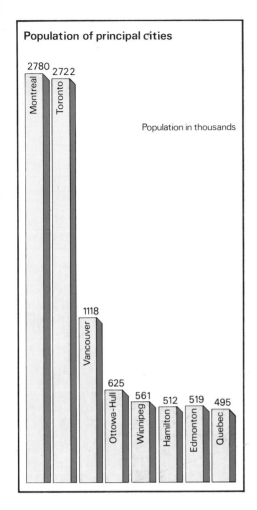

Population in thousands

- Montreal 2780
- Toronto 2722
- Vancouver 1118
- Ottowa-Hull 625
- Winnipeg 561
- Hamilton 512
- Edmonton 519
- Quebec 495

Population density

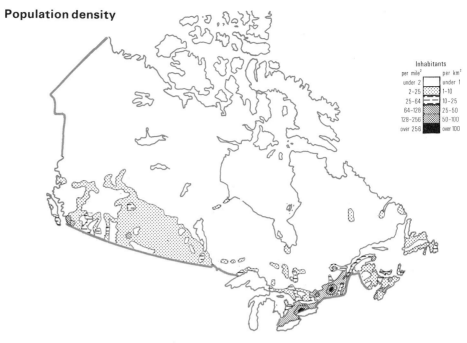

Inhabitants

per mile²	per km²
under 2	under 1
2–25	1–10
25–64	10–25
64–128	25–50
128–256	50–100
over 256	over 100

Population Distribution

The population of Canada is unevenly distributed. Most Canadians live within 100 miles of the U.S. border, in 16 of the 21 cities over 100,000. Sixty per cent of the population lives in the 600 miles between Quebec city and Windsor, Ontario—less than two per cent of the country's area. The north has less than 250,000 people, and the far north inside the Arctic Circle less than 20,000 people, most of whom are Eskimos. People tend to gravitate to southern Ontario cities and to British Columbia.

Government

Canada is a federal union and a constitutional monarchy. The Statute of Westminster in 1931 brought complete autonomy and equality with Britain, to which Canada was bound only by allegiance to the Crown.

Canada's constitution is based on the British North America Act (1867) and statutes of both the British and Canadian parliaments. The Canadian parliamentary system is based on that of the U.K. There is a central government in Ottawa, and each province has its own Premier and legislature. The *Crown* is represented by the *Governor-General*, who unifies the three branches of government. He is appointed on the advice of the Prime Minister. Although his function is largely ceremonial, he can dissolve parliament, usually at the government's request. The *Senate* is also appointed on the P.M.'s advice. It has an equal voice with the House of Commons in legislation, except that dealing with public funds and taxes. The *House of Commons* has an elected representation based on population and adjusted every 10 years. Elections are called at least every five years.

The *Prime Minister* is the leader of the party which has the largest number of seats in the House. He and his *Cabinet* are the executive of the government. If a bill proposed by the government is defeated, or if there is a vote of no-confidence, the government must resign.

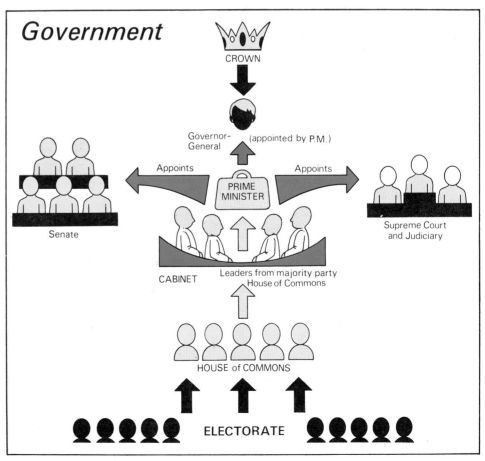

Government

CROWN

Governor-General (appointed by P.M.)

Appoints — PRIME MINISTER — Appoints

Senate

Supreme Court and Judiciary

CABINET — Leaders from majority party House of Commons

HOUSE of COMMONS

ELECTORATE

Reference

History

Main events in Canadian history

1000 Herjulf, a Norseman, visits Canadian coast. Leif Ericson spends winter in Vineland

1398 Sinclair, the Earl of Orkney explores Atlantic coast

1492 Columbus lands on Bahamas

1497 John Cabot discovers Canada's east coast while looking for the route to China.

1501 Caspar Corte-Real visits Newfoundland and Labrador for Portugal.

1524 Verrazano, an Italian working for France, explores coasts of Nova Scotia and Newfoundland

1524-42 Jacques Cartier's four voyages to Newfoundland, Gaspé, down the St. Lawrence to Quebec City and Montreal

1542-3 Sieur de Roberval's attempted settlement on the St. Lawrence fails

1577 Sir Martin Frobisher makes first of three voyages to discover the Northwest Passage

1583 Sir Humphrey Gilbert visits Newfoundland, England's first overseas colony and the beginning of the British Empire

1585 John Davis made first of three voyages for the Northwest Passage

1608 Samuel de Champlain founds Quebec City

1610 Henry Hudson explores Hudson Bay

1615 Champlain visits the Ottawa River, Georgian Bay, the Huron country and Lake Ontario

1629 Quebec captured by British adventurers and later restored

1631 Fox and James explore Hudson Bay

1634-41 Discovery and exploration of Great Lakes. Jean Nicolet (Michigan); Chaumonot and Brebeuf (Erie); Raymbault and Jogues (Superior).

1642 Montreal founded by Sieur de Maisonneuve

1649 Murder of Jesuits Brebeuf and Lalemant by Iroquois near Midland;

1659 Radisson and Groseilliers explore country near Lake Superior and possibly James Bay

1663 New France proclaimed Royal province by Louis XIV

1670 Hudson's Bay Company granted Royal Charter

1673 Fort Frontenac built by Frontenac

1678 Niagara Falls visited by Hennepin

1679 La Salle's *Le Griffon* built on Niagara River and first ship to sail Great Lakes

1682 La Salle descends the Mississippi to its mouth

1689-90 Last Iroquois War

1700 Compagnie du Canada formed to manage fur trade

1731 La Vérendrye begins western explorations and sights western mountains in 1743

1755 The expulsion of the Acadians, the original French settlers of Nova Scotia

1756 Declaration of Seven Years' War between Great Britain and France

1758 Louisbourg captured by British, the strongest citadel in North America on Cape Breton Island

1759 Wolfe defeats Montcalm on Plains of Abraham. Quebec surrenders to the British

1763 Treaty of Paris ends Seven Years' War; French positions in North America ceded to Britain with the exception of two islands

1770-72 Hearne's journey to the Coppermine and Slave Rivers and Great Slave Lake

1774 Passage of Quebec Act

1775 American Revolution

1776 Carleton defeats Americans who are driven from Canada

1778 James Cook explores Nootka Sound

1783 Immigration of United Empire Loyalists from the Thirteen Colonies

1791 Constitutional Act or Canada Act creating Upper and Lower Canada

1795 Pacific coast of Canada ceded to British by Spaniards

1807 David Thompson crosses Rockies. Death of Joseph Brant, famous Mohawk Indian chief

1808 Simon Fraser explores Fraser River to its mouth on Pacific — 850 miles.

1812 U.S. declares war against Britain and Canada. Death of General Brock at Queenston Heights

1813 Death of Tecumseh, Shawnee Indian chief who fought with British

Toronto burned by Americans

1814 Washington burned by British. Treaty ends war and fighting finishes in following year

1817 Rush-Bagot Convention with U.S. limiting naval armament on Great Lakes

1829 First Welland Canal opened

1831 North Magnetic Pole discovered by James Ross

1832 Opening of Rideau Canal

1836 First railway opened

1837 Rebellions in Upper and Lower Canada led by William Lyon Mackenzie and Louis Joseph Papineau

1838 Lord Durham sent out as extraordinary governor. Brings out his Durham Report recommending self-government.

1840 James Evans, a Methodist missionary in Manitoba, invents alphabet for Cree Indians

1841 Act of Union combines Upper and Lower Canada under one government; to be called Canada East and West

1843 Sir James Douglas builds Fort Victoria and earns title "Father of British Columbia"

1844 Charles Fenerty discovers practicable method of making paper from ground wood pulp

1845 Sir John Franklin disappears in Arctic

1846 Dr. Abraham Gesner of Nova Scotia discovers process for distilling kerosene from albertite

1847 Alexander Graham Bell born in Edinburgh; family moved to Brantford, Ont. in 1870 and Bell invented telephone there in 1874. Lord Elgin arrives as Governor-General to try responsible government

1849 Mob burns Parliament building over issue of compensation for rebels

1848 First Responsible Government in British Empire formed in Nova Scotia

1853 Opening of Grand Trunk Railway from Montreal to Portland

1857 Queen Victoria names Ottawa as national capital. North America's first oil well dug by James Miller Williams at Oil Springs, Ont.

1858 Decimal currency introduced. Atlantic cable completed. Gold Rush to Fraser River and new colony, British Columbia, formed; Vancouver Island colony united with it in 1866

1866 Fenians invade Canada from U.S. near Fort Erie, Ont.; repulsed by militia

1867 Confederation of Canada, N.S., N.B. as the Dominion of Canada. Russia sold Alaska to U.S.; boundary dispute with U.S. settled in 1903 when Britain acting on Canada's behalf gave way to Roosevelt's pressure

1868 D'Arcy McGee murdered by Fenian. Canada's only political assassination

1869 Transfer of Rupert's Land to the Dominion. Red River Rebellion led by Louis Riel. Seager Wheeler born and in 1904 begins breeding hard spring wheat

1870 Paper money issued, known as shin-plasters

1873 North West Mounted Police established

1876 Opening of Intercolonial Railway from Quebec to Halifax

1885 Second Riel rebellion; Riel executed. Last spike of Canadian Pacific Railway driven at Craigallachie, B.C.

1896	Gold discovered in Klondike by George Carmack; rush to Dawson starts following year
1901	Marconi receives first trans-Atlantic wireless message at St. John's, Nfld.
1903	Silver found in Cobalt, Ontario
1906	Roald Amundsen crosses the North-West Passage; Sir Robert M'Clure discovered passage in 1853
1907	Start of Quebec Bridge, world's longest single cantilever span, 1,800 feet
1914-18	World War I First Canadian Contingent of 33,000 troops landed in Plymouth in 1915 then Flanders
1917	Women granted right to vote in federal elections
1919	Winnipeg General Strike
1923	Sir Frederick Banting wins Nobel Prize for his 1921 discovery of insulin
1927	Diamond Jubilee of Confederation
1930	Source of uranium discovered near Great Bear Lake, N.W.T.
1931	Statute of Westminster
1935	March on Ottawa by unemployed broken up by R.C.M.P.
1939	Canada declares war on Germany
1942	National Selective Service announced. Aug. 19 Raid on Dieppe by Canadian troops with Allied support; 3,350 casualties out of 5,000. R.C.M.P. schooner St. Roch arrives at Halifax after sailing the Northwest Passage from Vancouver
1945	End of World War II 1,086,771 Canadians in forces
1946	Royal Commission to investigate Russian espionage after defection of Igor Gouzenko. Famous N.S. schooner Bluenose sinks
1950	Establishment of Alert, joint Canada-U.S. weather station, the farthest north, permanent human habitation in world
1953	Korean armistice; 27,000 Canadians fought in war which started in 1950
1957	DEW (Distant Early Warning) Line established by Canadian and U.S. air defences
1962	Canadian satellite Alouette launched for ionosphere study
1967	Researchers of the Royal Ontario Museum find artifacts near Medicine Hat, Alta. showing man lived in North America 30,000 years ago. Expo 67 at Montreal
1970	Following kidnappings and killings by Front de Liberation Québécois separatists, the controversial War Measures Act is passed; many arrests, followed by compensation.
1976	Parti Québécois elected to power in Quebec; pledged to make Quebec an independent state. Olympic Games held in Montreal.

The Arts

Time was when much of Canada's talent remained unsung abroad. Today, however, many of her artists and intellects are internationally respected. Canadian academics have followings at home and overseas: **Marshall McLuhan**, famous for his observations on the cultural aspects of communication; **Northrop Frye**, an influential Jungian literary critic; **John Kenneth Galbraith**, the economist and personality; and historians like **Donald Creighton, Harold Innis** and **Frank Underhill. Karsh** has photographed the world's famous faces, and the *Group of Seven* (original members **F. H. Varley, A. Y. Jackson, Lawren Harris, F. H. Johnston, Frank Carmichael, Arthur Lismer** and **J. E. H. MacDonald**) has painted the Canadian landscape with bold, original strokes. Novelists such as **Margaret Laurence** (*A Jest of God*) and **Mordecai Richler** (*The Apprenticeship of Duddy Kravitz*) have had their work translated into film. The following is a partial list of some well-known Canadians.

ARTISTS

Emily Carr (1871-1945) Painter and writer; studied in San Francisco, London and Paris; taught in Vancouver; famous for her original paintings of West Coast Indian life and British Columbian forests.

Lawren Harris (1885-1970) Originally a landscapist, turned to non-objective compositions; instrumental in the formation of the *Group of Seven*.

Paul Kane (1810-1871) Painter of Indian life. Born in Ireland and brought to Toronto when ten; studied in U.S. and Europe, travelled as far as the Pacific Northwest sketching Indian life.

Cornelius Kreighoff (1812-72) Born in Holland, official U.S. war artist with U.S. army during Seminole War; opened studio in Toronto in 1846, moved to Quebec where he painted local scenes.

Robert Tait Mackenzie (1867-1938) Professor of anatomy at McGill; medical research led to art. Untaught sculptor he produced over 200 outstanding works.

WRITERS

Thomas Chandler Haliburton (1796-1865) especially noted for his Sam Slick papers; Canada's first internationally known humorist.

L. M. Montgomery (1874-1942) childhood classic, the world-famous *Anne of Green Gables* has been a bestseller for over fifty years.

Stephen Leacock (1869-1944) Canada's best loved humorist see *Sunshine Sketches of a Little Town*.

Mazo de la Roche (1879-1961) large international following of her *Jalna* series.

Ringuet (1895-1960) pen name of Dr. Phillipe Panneton. Many novels; most famous *Trente Arpents* (Thirty Acres).

Pierre Berton (b. 1920) well-known journalist, author and director. See *The National Dream* on Canada's railways.

POETS

John McCrae (1872-1918) a Canadian doctor, is famous for one poem, "In Flanders Fields".

Francois-Xavier Garneau. His *Histoire du Canada*, (1845-8) gave a nationist impetus to French-Canadian poetry.

E. Pauline Johnson (1862-1913) called *Tekahionwake*. Canada's best-known Indian writer.

Saint-Denys Garneau (1916-43) abstract and symbolic poetry.

E. J. Pratt (1883-1964) probably the country's best-known poet. He is surely its most adventurous. *Witches Brew* (1926), *The Fable of the Goats* (1937), *Brébeuf and His Brethren* (1940).

Leonard Cohen (b. 1934) romantic poet and singer with large following of young people.

Science and Industry

Sir Frederick Banting (1891-1941) discovered insulin and its effect on diabetes in 1921 at the University of Toronto, with **Dr. Charles Best** he won a Nobel Prize in 1923.

Alexander Graham Bell (1847-1922) invented the telephone in Brantford, Ontario, in 1874; he invented the gramophone record and photophone, forerunner of film sound track and electric eye, he also made flight experiments.

Dr. Norman Bethune (1899-1939) was a famous surgeon, renowned for his work in China.

Samuel Cunard (1787-1865) was the founder of the Cunard Line, the world's largest ships; he was the son of a Halifax master carpenter.

James Evans (1801-1846) was a Methodist minister in Manitoba who invented the syllabic alphabet for the Cree Indians and printed a hymn book on birch bark (invented in 1840). His alphabet is now used by Indians in most of the north.

Sir Sandford Fleming (1827-1915) was a civil engineer whose Standard Time System in 1884 was adopted by North American railways.

Dr. Abraham Gesner (1797-1864) discovered how to distil kerosene from albertite in 1846, the start of modern petroleum refining.

Robert Samuel Mclaughlin (1872-1972), or "Colonel Sam", was a pioneer of the North American automobile industry, and a noted designer and philanthropist.

Sir William Osler (1849-1919) was a medical educator—called the father of psychosomatic medicine, he revolutionized the treatment of patients and in 1887 headed the medical school at John Hopkins University.

Reference
The Economy

FACTS AND FIGURES
Gross national product (1974):
$140 billion.
Per Capita GNP $6,170.
Growth rate: 5% estimated for 1976.
Main sources of income:
Manufacturing: Canada ranks
sixth in the world. Motor vehicles,
chemical products, textiles and
clothing, electrical products, iron,
steel, lumber, processing of agricultural and fishery products.
Agriculture: Wheat and grains,
sugar beets, tobacco, potatoes, fruits,
bulbs and seeds, vegetables, livestock.
Forest industries: world's largest
accessible wood supply. Pulp, news-
print, fine papers, building material,
plastics, cellophane, rayon and raw
textile materials.
Mining and energy resources:
petroleum, coal, natural gas, electric
power, sixty minerals.
Other sources: fur, fisheries,
construction and services.
Currency: the dollar (floating):
£1 equals $1.66 (June 1976)

Deflation and Diversity

Canada is a prosperous country with a very
high standard of living. Although somewhat
sheltered, she too is just emerging from a
smaller version of the recession. In the
future she will no doubt try to expand her
manufacturing and reduce her dependence
on exporting raw materials and energy.
Wages in manufacturing have increased,
while productivity has not—a situations
which does not make Canada as competitive
as she might wish to be especially with the
U.S. She is also trying to diversify her
economic links especially in Europe.

At home inflation and 7% unemployment
remain problems. After slow growth in 1974,
the Gross National Product will not rise in
1975 and it appears that the balance of
merchandise trade will go against Canada
throughout the year. In October 1975 the
Trudeau government announced an anti-
inflation programme discouraging wage
increases over 10%. This long awaited
leadership may prove difficult to implement,
however, and it remains to be seen how the
county will react. The near future will probably witness neither boom nor bust. Fore-
casters agree on a real growth of about 5% in
1976. Incomes are still rising. Partial indexing
of income taxes and generous unemployment
benefits ease inflation and unemployment.
Canada is not alone in the fight against
inflation and she is thankful for her "good
life".

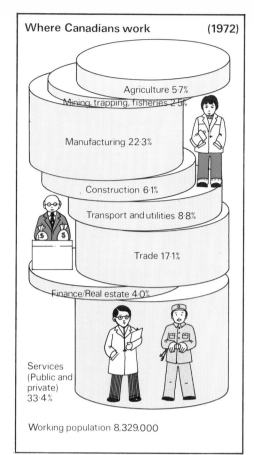

Where Canadians work (1972)

Agriculture 5·7%
Mining, trapping, fisheries 2·5%
Manufacturing 22·3%
Construction 6·1%
Transport and utilities 8·8%
Trade 17·1%
Finance/Real estate 4·0%
Services (Public and private) 33·4%

Working population 8,329,000

Potatoes
Sugar Beet
Apples
Grapes
Wheat
Oats
Maize
Barley
Flax
Tobacco

Edmonton
Vancouver
Calgary
Regina
Winnipeg
Quebec
Montreal
Ottawa
Toronto
Windsor

Agriculture in Canada

Cattle
Dairy Products
Pigs
Sheep
Fur Trapping Areas
Principle Fishing Areas & Ports

Industry in Canada

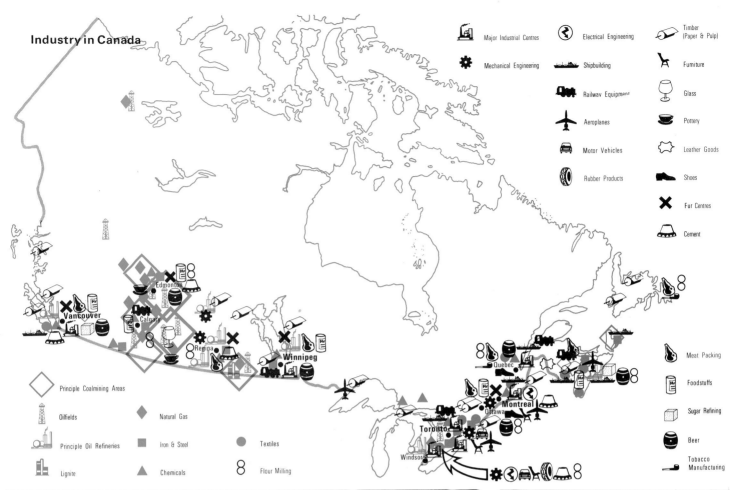

	Major Industrial Centres
	Mechanical Engineering
	Railway Equipment
	Aeroplanes
	Motor Vehicles
	Rubber Products
	Electrical Engineering
	Shipbuilding
	Timber (Paper & Pulp)
	Furniture
	Glass
	Pottery
	Leather Goods
	Shoes
	Fur Centres
	Cement
	Meat Packing
	Foodstuffs
	Sugar Refining
	Beer
	Tobacco Manufacturing

Principle Coalmining Areas
Oilfields
Principle Oil Refineries
Lignite
Natural Gas
Iron & Steel
Chemicals
Textiles
Flour Milling

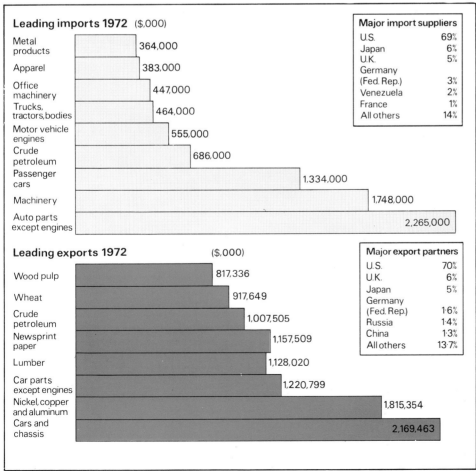

Leading imports 1972 ($,000)

Metal products	364,000
Apparel	383,000
Office machinery	447,000
Trucks, tractors, bodies	464,000
Motor vehicle engines	555,000
Crude petroleum	686,000
Passenger cars	1,334,000
Machinery	1,748,000
Auto parts except engines	2,265,000

Major import suppliers

U.S.	69%
Japan	6%
U.K.	5%
Germany (Fed. Rep.)	3%
Venezuela	2%
France	1%
All others	14%

Leading exports 1972 ($,000)

Wood pulp	817,336
Wheat	917,649
Crude petroleum	1,007,505
Newsprint paper	1,157,509
Lumber	1,128,020
Car parts except engines	1,220,799
Nickel, copper and aluminum	1,815,354
Cars and chassis	2,169,463

Major export partners

U.S.	70%
U.K.	6%
Japan	5%
Germany (Fed. Rep.)	1.6%
Russia	1.4%
China	1.3%
All others	13.7%

Percentage of household conveniences in Canada (1972)

Electricity	99%
Running water	98%
Central heating	87%
Radios	98%
Powered washing machines	79%
Telephones	95%
Mechanical refrigerators	99%
Powered lawnmowers	57%
Electric/gas ranges	93%
Cars	78%
More than one car	18%
Television sets	96%

What is owned compared to other nations

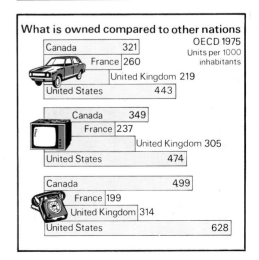

OECD 1975
Units per 1000 inhabitants

Canada	321
France	260
United Kingdom	219
United States	443

Canada	349
France	237
United Kingdom	305
United States	474

Canada	499
France	199
United Kingdom	314
United States	628

Gazetteer

PROVINCES AND TERRITORIES

Alberta (area: 255,285 sq. miles, population: 1,627,874) Its warm summers and cold winters are moderated by the Chinook wind. Noted for farming and oil, particularly along the Athabasca River; the sands there are the largest single reserve of oil known to man, but difficult to exploit.

British Columbia (area: 2,184,621 sq. miles, population: 2,452,000) Mild climate; forestry dominates, though mining is catching up. Fruit and fishing also famous.

Manitoba (area: 251,000 sq. miles, population: 1,016,000) Wheat industry began here. Has the largest nickel-producing complex in the world at Thompson and the continent's largest tantalum mine. Warm summers and very cold winters.

New Brunswick (area: 28,354 sq. miles, population: 673,000) Continental climate, moderated by the sea. First coal mines to be worked in North America. Fishing and farming, leading potato producer. Originally part of French Arcadia.

Newfoundland (area: 156,185 sq. miles, population: 548,000) Includes Island of Newfoundland and Labrador. Cold Labrador current affects the otherwise moderating sea influence on climate. Fishing and logging predominate; ship-building also important. Much revenue comes in from foreign fishing fleets.

Northwest Territories (area: 1,304,904 sq. miles, population: 37,000) Coldest part of Canada. Only the southern part is outside permafrost zone; summers last about three months. Main industries are mining, fur, fishing and oil exploration.

Nova Scotia (area: 21,425 sq. miles, population: 821,000) Rich soil produces highest yield per acre in Canada. Noted for its apple orchards in the Annapolis Valley. First in fisheries production.

Ontario (area: 412,582 sq. miles, population: 8,200,000) Cold winters, warm summers with milder temperatures on the Niagara Peninsula. Biggest wealth producer; most industrialized, most urbanized of provinces. While it also has the largest number of occupied farms, 20 million acres of virgin agricultural land exists.

Prince Edward Island (2,184 sq. miles, population: 119,000) Called "Garden of the Gulf" because of its moderate climate and fertile soil; noted for potatoes.

Quebec (area: 594,860 sq. miles, population: 6,176,000) Largest of the ten provinces, with a variety of climates. Farming important, first in pulp and paper production. Shares Ungava iron ore deposits with Newfoundland. Richest province in water power resources. "La Belle Province" is French Canada's centre.

Saskatchewan (area: 251,700 sq. miles, population: 915,000) Noted for its wheat. Largest area of occupied agricultural land in Canada.

The Yukon Territories (area: 207,076 sq. miles, population: 21,000) Mineral resources, water power resources. Famous for gold rush of 1896.

NATIONAL CAPITAL

Ottawa (45 25N 75 43W) Pop. 302,341; metropolitan area pop. 453,280. Selected as Canada's capital in 1854. Points of interest include the Parliament buildings, Byward Market, National Gallery, National Archives and Arts centre. Often spoken of as Ottawa-Hull. **Hull** (45 26N 74 45W) has metropolitan population of 149,230.

PROVINCIAL AND TERRITORIAL CAPITALS

Charlottetown (46 14N 63 9W) Pop. 19,133. Capital of Prince Edward Island. Deep water harbour and commercial centre for province. 1864 meeting here led to Canadian Federation.

Edmonton (53 34N 113 25W) Pop. 438,152. Capital of Alberta. Refining centre and pipeline terminus.

Fredericton (45 57N 66 40W) Pop. 24,254. Capital of New Brunswick. The "Poet's Corner of Canada", main distributing centre for province and commercial hunting and fishing depot.

Halifax (44 38N 63 35W) Pop. 122,035. Capital of Nova Scotia. Canada's chief Atlantic coast port, ice-free in winter. Seven-mile long harbour.

Quebec City (46 50N 71 15W) Pop. 1,214,352; metropolitan area pop: 480,502. Capital of Quebec province. Important seaport and picturesque city. Canada's oldest, and North America's only fortified city.

Regina (50 30N 104 38W) Pop. 139,469. Capital of Saskatchewan. Midway across the prairies; Royal Canadian Mounted Police headquarters, one of the world's largest distributing centres for farm implements.

St. John's (47 34N 52 41W) Pop: 89,039. Capital of Newfoundland. Fine harbour; first transatlantic wireless message received here by Marconi; first non-stop transatlantic flight began here also.

Toronto (43 42N 79 25W) Pop: 712,786. Metropolitan area pop: 2,628,043. Capital of Ontario. Financial and commercial centre second only to Montreal in manufacturing; cultural centre.

Victoria (48 26N 123 20W) Pop. 61,761. Capital of British Columbia. Fishing fleet headquarters; fine public buildings, English atmosphere.

Whitehorse (60 41N 135 8W) Pop. 21,000. Capital of the Yukon Territory. Began in gold rush; distribution and communications centre for the Yukon.

Winnipeg (49 53N 97 10W) Pop. 246,246. Capital of Manitoba, at junction of Assiniboine and Red Rivers. Famous for its general strike of 1921.

Yellowknife (62 30N 114 29W) Pop. 6,122. Capital of the Northwest Territories. Established as gold mining town. Name comes from the Yellowknife Indians who used copper tools.

OTHER PRINCIPAL CITIES

Calgary (51 0N 114 10W) Alberta. In the foothills of the Rockies, surrounded by farms, ranches and oil wells. The biggest rodeo in the world takes place every year in July at the Calgary Stampede.

Hamilton (43 20N 79 50W) Ontario "Steel City of Canada" located at the western edge of Lake Ontario.

London (43 0N 81 15W) Ontario. Located in the valley of the Thames River. Place names in city include Pall Mall, Trafalgar, Piccadilly and Hyde Park.

Montreal (45 31N 73 34W) Quebec. Pop. 2,743,208. Canada's largest city. A huge, cosmopolitan city, ⅔ of it French-speaking. Superb subway, many parks, Palais des arts.

St. John (45 20N 66 8W) New Brunswick. The province's second largest city, dating to 1631. The tides of the Bay of Fundy flow in and out of mouth of St. John River, causing mighty Reversing Falls.

Vancouver (49 20N 123 10W) British Columbia. Canada's third largest city, with a metropolitan population of over one million. The hub of Western Canada.

PRINCIPAL RIVERS

Mackenzie River (including tributaries)	2,635 miles
Yukon River (to Pacific Ocean)	1,979 miles
St. Lawrence River (to Atlantic)	1,900 miles
Nelson River (to Hudson Bay)	1,600 miles
Saskatchewan River (to Hudson Bay)	1,205 miles
Pearce River (to Arctic Ocean)	1,195 miles
Churchill River (to Hudson Bay)	1,000 miles

PRINCIPAL MOUNTAINS

Mount Logan (Yukon)	19,850 ft.
Mount Fairweather (British Columbia)	15,300 ft.
Mount Waddington (British Columbia)	13,260 ft.
Mount Robson (British Columbia)	12,972 ft.
Mount Columbia (Alberta)	12,294 ft.

Index

CANADA Physical

Cities and Towns ◉ ◎ ○ ○

International Boundaries

Ice Cap

Mountain Peaks (feet) ▲ 13,905

metres	2743	1829	914	305	152	0
feet	9000	6000	3000	1000	500	0

Below sea level

Scale 1:21,000,000

300 miles
400 kilometres
0 100 200 300
0 100 200 300 400

Projection : Oblique Conic

GREENLAND

Mt. Forel 11,100

Godhaab

Christianshaab

Sukkertoppen

Upernivik

Arctic Circle

Thule

Davis Strait

Disko I.

Baffin Bay

BEAUFORT SEA

Brooks Range

Arctic Circle

Fort Yukon

Fairbanks

Valdez

U.S.A.

Mt. McKinley 20,320

Whitehorse

Dawson

Yukon

Mt. St. Elias 18,008

Mt. Logan 19,850

Juneau

Mt. Fairweather 15,300

Gulf of Alaska

Wrangell

Prince Rupert

Alexander Archipelago

Queen Charlotte Islands

Hecate Str.

PACIFIC OCEAN

Pt. Patrick

Pr. Alfred C.

Banks Island

McClure Strait

Melville I.

Bathurst I.

Viscount Melville Sound

Resolute

Pr. of Wales I.

Victoria Island

Cambridge Bay

Amundsen Gulf

C. Bathurst

Inuvik

Fort Good Hope

Mackenzie Mountains

Selwyn Mts.

Stikine

Coast Mountains

Fraser

Prince George

Kamloops

Vancouver Island

Victoria

C. Flattery

Tacoma

Seattle

Mt. Rainier 14,410

Axel Heiberg I.

Ellesmere Island

Devon Island

Lancaster Sound

Somerset Island

Queen Elizabeth Islands

G. of Boothia

Spence Bay

Garry Lake

Bathurst Inlet

Coppermine

Gt. Bear Lake

Gt. Slave Lake

Yellowknife

Hay River

Caribou Mts.

Birch Mts.

Peace

Lesser Slave Lake

Athabasca

Lake Athabasca

Uranium City

Fond du Lac

Reindeer Lake

Lake Manitoba

Dawson Creek

Churchill Pk. 9,971

Yellowhead Pass

Salkirk Mts.

Selkirk Mts.

Kicking Horse Pass

Edmonton

Calgary

Crowsnest Pass

Banff

Lethbridge

Medicine Hat

Swift Current

Regina

Moose Jaw

Brandon

Saskatoon

Prince Albert

Saskatchewan

L. Winnipegosis

L. Manitoba

Portage la Prairie

Winnipeg

St. Boniface

Red

Grand Forks

Bismark

Pierre

UNITED STATES

Black Hills

Billings

Great Falls

Butte

Helena

Boise

Casper

Cheyenne

Denver

Salt Lake City

Ogden

Reno

Sacramento

Oakland

San Francisco

Mt. Shasta 14,162

Eugene

Salem

Portland

Spokane

BAFFIN ISLAND

Frobisher Bay

Cumberland Sound

Mt. Logan

C. Chidley

Nain

Hopedale

Hudson Strait

Wakeham

Suglukl

Port Harrison

Ungava Bay

Fort Chimo

Nouveau Quebec

C. Chidley

Labrador

Hebron

Battle Harbour

Belle Isle Str.

Hudson Bay

Foxe Basin

Mansel I.

Coats I.

Ottawa Is.

Belcher Is.

James Bay

C. Henrietta Maria

Akimiski I.

Fort George

Fort Albany

Moosonee

Eastmain

Gt. Whale

Leaf

Schefferville

Wabush

Lake Michikamau

Hamilton

Lake Melville

Grand Falls

Gander

Newfoundland

St. John's

Bonavista

Chesterfield Inlet

Eskimo Point

C. Churchill

York

Port Nelson

Churchill

Seal

Nelson

Lynn Lake

C. Tatnam

Fort Severn

Severn

Sioux Lookout

Nipigon

Lake Nipigon

Hearst

Kapuskasing

Timmins

Rouyn

Chibougamau

Chicoutimi

Jonquière

Lake Mistassini

Eastmain

Lake St. Jean

Trois Rivières

Montreal

Hull

OTTAWA

Quebec

St. Hyacinthe

Lewis

Edmundston

Fredericton

Saint John

B. of Fundy

Moncton

Edward I.

Charlottetown

Bathurst

Bas. St.

Anticosti I.

Gulf of St. Lawrence

Gaspé

St. Lawrence

Rimouski

Sydney

Cape Breton I.

Cabot Str.

ST. PIERRE (Fr.)

MIQUELON (Fr.)

Halifax

Yarmouth

C. Sable

Port aux Basques

Corner Brook

Kenora

Fort Frances

Duluth

St. Paul

Minneapolis

Sioux Falls

Sioux City

Cedar Rapids

Des Moines

Omaha

Lincoln

Thunder Bay

Sault Ste. Marie

Michipicoten Harbour

Lake Superior

Sudbury

North Bay

Owen Sound

Georgian Bay

Orillia

Toronto

Hamilton

Kitchener

London

Windsor

Detroit

Toledo

Akron

Cleveland

Lake Huron

Lake Michigan

Lake Erie

Green Bay

Bay City

Flint

Lansing

Grand Rapids

Milwaukee

Madison

Chicago

Gary

UNITED STATES OF AMERICA

Buffalo

Rochester

Syracuse

Utica

Albany

Hartford

New Haven

New York

Newark

Scranton

Pittsburgh

Kingston

Oshawa

Providence

Boston

C. Cod

Portland

Augusta

ATLANTIC OCEAN

West of Greenwich

ROCKY Mountains

Mackenzie

Horn Mts.

Coppermine

Liard

Peace

3 4 5 6 7 8 9 10-CAD-81 80